W9-ABI-816

Building Productivity

Blueprints For Success

National Science Foundation Library

National Science Foundation library

Building Productivity

Blueprints For Success

by Eileen Berman, Ed.D.

Authority Press Inc.

HD
56
.B47
2000

© 2000 Authority Press Inc.
All rights reserved. Published by Authority Press Inc. No part of this
book may be reproduced in any form without written permission
from the Publisher. The views and concepts presented are those of
the contributors. Publication by Authority Press Inc. does not in any
way constitute endorsement or approval of the book's contents. No
responsibility is assumed by the Publisher for any injury and/or
damage to persons or property as a matter of product's liability,
due to negligence or otherwise, or from any use or operation of any
methods, products, instructions, or ideas contained in the material
herein.

Printed in the United States of America.

03   02   01   00   1   2   3   4   5

Library of Congress Catalog Number: 99-64572

ISBN 1-929059-00-0

Authority Press Inc.
10970 Morton's Crossing
Alpharetta, GA 30022
770-475-2837
www.authoritypress.com

Publisher: Eric E. Torrey
Editor: Elizabeth P. Gordon
Cover: Craig Hall, Streambed Graphics
Printer: Sheridan Books

Dedication

To:
Stan, Jo, Andy, and Kiwi.

With Love!

ENDORSEMENTS

Bill McGovern
Vice President, Human Resources
Wyman-Gordon Company

Employing her signature style of analogies related to building and construction, Dr. Eileen Berman furnishes the reader with two sets of blueprints for success. The first set guides the manager in his or her efforts to build a committed and productive team of employees. The second set of blueprints is a self-help guide for anyone who is striving to balance a productive career with an equally-important focus on family, emotional well-being and responsibility to the world around us. I predict that *Building Productivity: 18 Blueprints for Success* will be the primer for win-win employment relationships far into the next century.

Joseph C. Formichelli
Executive Vice-President
Toshiba America Information Systems

Although the world is changing at a very rapid pace, Dr. Berman reminds us in her very readable book, *Building Productivity*, that the basic elements of any successful business haven't changed. People are still the heart and soul of every organization. A must-read for every employee who cares to make a difference.

Nathan Morton
Chairman of the Board
BuildNet, Inc.

There is no comparison to the contribution each person can make if they truly *want* to do something instead of *having* to do something. Dr. Berman offers valuable insight and practical reality that allows organizations to fully involve the workforce while allowing each individual a clear path to success, job satisfaction and personal well-being, as the company benefits. A great book for anyone in business to read."

Thomas F. Jenkins
Plant Manger, Superabrasives
Norton Company

18 Blueprints is an easy read -- it's fast-paced and concise. Any manager, newly appointed or experienced, who wants to do a better job of communicating and increase his groups' productivity can utilize this book. The use of individual project plans at the end of each chapter makes this a great reference and teaching tool. *Sound advice -- Pay Attention!*

Patricia A. Viscardi, R.N., B.S.N.
President and CEO
Case Management Services

As an occupational health professional, I can attest to the impact of stress on workplace performance. Dr. Berman is right on target with her emphasis on the "soft skills." By using the techniques and guidelines outlined in this book, managers will empower their people to achieve higher levels of personal and professional growth. I read every word of *Building Productivity* and loved it!

TABLE OF CONTENTS

AN
INTRODUCTION

Every manager knows that improving productivity is a priority. Without competitive cost output, a business will die. In this book, the author is not talking about material output, although that will be a by-product. She is concerned about the ability of the employee to be involved in an environment that promotes the freedom to produce. She is talking about creating employee optimization.

To optimize someone's performance is to help that individual function as effectively as possible and contribute to the success of the organization. Building productivity is an ongoing quest; it is never finished, it is not static. The question is – Who is responsible for creating an environment in which productivity can occur? What are the blueprints for building this type of organization?

The first letters of the words **C**reating **E**mployee **O**ptimization spell CEO. An effective CEO motivates, leads, supports, and educates. If he succeeds at these tasks, he will create a system of optimization that will have a profound and positive impact on the company. However, these tasks are not only the responsibility of the chief executive officer. They are also part of the job description of every manager and supervisor. Creating an environment for employee optimization is an intrinsic part of a leader's job. The problem is that most people do not come by these skills naturally, nor are they exposed to this type of learning as part of a specific discipline. Although executives may be adept in their field of study, they may not be as skillful in the human dimension of business.

In order for businesses to be productive, they have to create a climate of vitality, newness, trust and openness, in which employees are encouraged to think, learn, and express themselves. As people participate more, they gain greater control over their lives. They begin to enjoy life more and feel less stress. *Building Productivity: 18 Blueprints for Success* is designed to help businesses create this type of atmosphere. The book addresses itself to the understanding of this concept so that people can gain greater control over their environment. In this way, businesses enhance productivity.

The blueprints in this book explore many of the "soft" skills necessary to create an environment in which productivity can occur. In reading and sharing them with their staff, people who supervise have the opportunity to add to their fund of knowledge about themselves and their relationships with others, so that they can affect their staff in ways that will promote growth. As their people grow, so will their business. By getting in touch with the qualities and skills that create effective teamwork, i.e., high morale, company identification and company loyalty, people will be better able to understand how to be productive. By being aware of the human dimension of business, management will enhance productivity – their own as well as that of their staff. The blueprints for building a successful business will help those in supervisory roles find the best in themselves and their people so that they and the company can profit. They will, in effect, be building productivity by creating employee optimization.

These blueprints appeared originally over a ten-year period as the *CEO GROWLETTERS*. Because of their success in promoting growth in organizations, they have been revised and published in their present form to help companies learn how to build productivity. To optimize the use of this book, there is a suggested plan for reading it. It is advisable to have an annual study plan, which will involve managers and their staffs to read and study one Blueprint per month. This will expose them to twelve Blueprints in the course of a year. Since there are eighteen Blueprints, it is not necessary to go in sequence, but to choose whichever ones are relevant to the department or company during that particular month.

Is it necessary to go beyond the reading stage? The fact that you read something does not motivate you to change and grow. This brings to mind a parallel with the way muscles work. When muscles are strained, they do not function well; thus they prevent you from being productive. In order to relieve them of stress, they need to be retaught. Only constant attention to these muscles can get them to begin to function optimally once again. And so it is with the mind and emotions, behaviors and attitudes. You have to begin to relearn and then reteach yourself if you are going to use all your resources – if you are going to be productive.

In much the same way, a company has to become aware of its weaknesses as well as its strengths. It has to begin the process of relearning. Its management must be open to discussing with their people how to effect changes in the organization in order to improve productivity. With this in mind, after each blueprint is a Project Plan, for the individual and the company, which consists of exercises to do in order to implement the contents of the blueprint.

Goals should be set and people encouraged to begin to make changes. The Blueprints are a guide to determine what is needed within the company to diminish stress and promote better relationships to enhance productivity. They are used to stimulate discussions among the staff, encouraging interaction, and they are the beginning for creating employee optimization. By utilizing the blueprints in this manner, accountability is also created, and accountability is a powerful catalyst for change. At the end of the year, companies are encouraged to measure their change to see how these blueprints have contributed to their productivity.

The illustrations referred to in several blueprints are composites of actual cases the author has dealt with over the years. All the cases have been sufficiently changed so that the people and the companies are unidentifiable.

The objective of this book is to teach people how to optimize their lives. It is concerned with the lessening of stress in order to enhance personal, and company, productivity. The thesis is that competence in any area of life helps reduce stress and builds productivity. The more competent a person is, the less anxiety she will feel. In other words, the *Blueprints for Success* are a means to educate, encourage, and inform the reader how to be more productive personally and professionally.

Dr. Berman is also the author of *Dealing Effectively With Job Loss: A Unique Approach To Rebuilding Your Life*. She conducts productivity and skills-building seminars for companies and writes a monthly column for *Industrial Management* magazine on the subject of productivity in the workplace.

THE IMPACT OF STRESS ON PRODUCTIVITY

When you say you are "under stress," what exactly do you mean? Are you feeling overwhelmed? Helpless? In control or out of control? Stress comes in different packages and, when at an uncomfortable level, can rob you of energy and creativity. It can even destroy relationships and jobs. In order to be productive, you must become aware of your own stress level and the negative stressors that are having an impact on your life.

To clear the record, not all stress is bad. There is "good" stress and there is "bad" stress. "Good" stress gives you just the added amount of adrenaline, energy, or excitement needed to get involved in life in a meaningful way. It adds zest and interest to daily living. It makes you feel alive. "Bad" stress, on the other hand, does just the opposite. It tends to present you with too much anxiety — too much adrenaline — so that your thinking may become clouded and unfocused, and physical symptoms such as shallow breathing, sweating, dry mouth, blurred vision, sleep and appetite disturbances may occur. Emotional distress in the form of irritability, mood swings, and difficulty concentrating may also be present. Therefore, when you talk about "bad" stress, you are really talking about distress...discomfort...negative feelings. What causes too much stress or distress? And what can you do about it?

THE THREE FACES OF STRESS

I like to think about stress as having three faces: inner, outer, and interpersonal. If you think of stress in this way, you will find it easier to get in touch with your own strengths and weaknesses, so you can begin to determine ways to perform more effectively.

The First Face

The *inner face* is your own intrinsic makeup, your own individual temperament, personality, and upbringing that make you you. Everyone is different. Some people are wound more tightly than others. Their nervous system is more sensitive and reactive to the world around them. They seem to feel more internally. Others appear calmer, more placid, not easily ruffled. They are able to deal with their feelings in such a way that no matter what the stressor, they usually continue to function in a productive way.

The Second Face

The *outer face* refers to the impact on you of the world in which you live. Where do you work? Is it a low-keyed place or a high-drive one? Is your work demanding? Do you have tight schedules to meet? Or are you involved mainly with projects with flexible due dates? What kind of home do you live in? Is it a highly-structured household, organized and run by the clock? Or is it a flexible, laissez-faire environment in which everyone does things with no schedules and few routines? Do you drive to work with barely any traffic, or do you struggle to keep the car at the speed limit as the traffic whizzes by you? In other words, what happens in the world around you defines the outer face of stress.

The Third Face

The *interpersonal face* has to do with interpersonal relations. When we talk about the interpersonal face of stress, we mean how you get along with other people and what their effect is on you. We'll talk more about this aspect of stress in the next Blueprint. In this Blueprint, we are going to confine ourselves to understanding the first two faces of stress.

THE INNER AND OUTER FACES OF STRESS

What is your inner stress level? How do you respond to being asked to stay late to finish a job? To being corrected? To being passed over for promotion? In order to help yourself grow, you have to know the triggers that cause stress to turn into distress. We are all unique, and we have to respect these individual differences in ourselves and others. For some people, it takes a lot to make them uncomfortable. For others, it takes very little. All of us do not react the same way to the same incidents. Different triggers set off different levels of stress.

By being aware of your own behavior, you will begin to understand what is going on around you and be able to deal with it more effectively. You will also be able to judge whether a fast-paced environment is something to which you can adapt, or whether your type of temperament would do better in a less demanding one.

To evaluate whether you are functioning at your comfort level, you need to step back and look at yourself. Are you enjoying yourself? Are you calm? Are you productive? Are you finding it difficult to concentrate? Are you getting little pleasure out of life? Are your relationships with your family members becoming difficult? Are you less tolerant of your friends and colleagues? Do you always seem to be in a rush? When you are driving, are you relaxed and willing to flow with what is out there, or are you uptight, blowing your horn, cussing the other drivers, and weaving in and out of traffic? Are you developing unhealthy behaviors, such as smoking and/or drinking a bit too much?

All these behaviors are signs of the outer face of stress affecting your inner face. How much can you tolerate? What circumstances cause you difficulty? What changes do you have to make in your living conditions in order to lower stress to an acceptable level?

It is either the environment you live in or work in which has an impact upon your own unique style of coping. Sometimes it is a job in which you may feel insecure and not up to the level of expertise required. Sometimes it is living above your means, so that indebtedness is a constant worry. Sometimes it is illness in someone you love, whom you are concerned about or feel powerless to help. Sometimes it is a relationship gone awry.

CHANGE

Change is a significant stressor. When you are faced with change, whether good or bad, you feel the impact of the outer face of stress. Change brings unfamiliarity. As a result, feelings of tension arise as you worry about what is in store for you. What will be the consequences of change? A promotion or a firing—one "good", one "bad"—can each bring its own high degree of stress. Marriage or divorce gives even more stress, although one can be considered "good" and the other "bad."

Even if you are aware of areas in your life that could use a bit of changing, you may be afraid of doing anything because the familiar may be preferable to the unknown. Old ways are like old friends: you may find fault with them, but you miss them when they are not around. It is a question of feeling safe and secure, and security and safety are tied up in predictability. With change, there is uncertainty and a sense of loss. Even though there may be significant gain to be had from the change, you may find yourself yearning for what you gave up. Your response clearly emanates both from your inner face of stress and from what the outer face is presenting.

YOUR PERCEPTION

Then there is the matter of perception — how you view things. Your inner face of stress is very much involved in how you interpret what is going on around you. How you view things determines how much stress you get from your environment. Everyone sees and interprets things in different ways. How you view what is going on depends on where you're coming from.

Some people might view a new job as very challenging and exciting. Other people might yearn for their old one because it was comfortable and predictable. Some people will climb mountains for the thrill of it; others won't leave their home because it feels safe.

In other words, stress to a great extent is in the eye of the beholder, as well as in his temperament and environment. How you view the outer face has to do with your inner face.

The following illustration is an example of both faces interacting with each other.

ILLUSTRATION

A few years ago, Richard, a young osteopath, came to me for help. He had just opened a new office and, instead of being energized at this new opportunity to practice independently, he was quite distraught and found going to work exceedingly difficult. Richard was in the business of making people well through manipulative techniques. Prior to his entering independent practice, he had worked very successfully in a group where he could call for help in his areas of weakness and give help to his colleagues in his areas of strength. His difficulties began when he decided to go into business for himself and by himself. Not only was he fearful about practicing alone, but his distress was compounded by the fact that he was deep in debt and worried about how he was going to meet his monthly mortgage payments.

I met Richard after he had been in his new office about two months. He came to me in a very anxious state. He could not sleep at night and every morning he felt a sense of panic when he thought of what lay ahead of him in his working day. This feeling didn't subside as the day wore on; it only got worse. He questioned his competence and began to worry that he might touch a patient in a way that would cause further injury. As he questioned his skills level, his doubts about himself rose enormously. He was anxiety-ridden and found it difficult to concentrate. Not only couldn't he sleep but his appetite was affected as well.

Soon he was losing patients. He feared having to manipulate them, and his patients were losing confidence in him. The messages he was sending — both spoken and unspoken — were not what you would call confidence-building. Soon he began to question whether he wanted to continue in his present profession. He was in a quandary about what he wished to do instead.

INNER FORCES vs. OUTER FORCES

This case is an example of the clash between inner forces and outer forces: the self vs. the environment. The impact of outer forces on Richard's limited inner forces was too much for him to manage. His stress level became too high for him to function effectively.

When Richard decided to open his own office, he may have thought he was far more skilled than he actually was. His weaknesses came to the surface when he became an independent practitioner and did not have the immediate support or advice of his fellow colleagues. When he decided to open up an independent practice, he saw only the benefits of being his own boss. He never anticipated the downside of being alone.

On another level, he was totally unaware of his emotional needs. Richard's lack of knowledge about himself kept him from realizing that he needed to have support and encouragement to function effectively. His need to be part of a group where he could feed his lack of confidence in himself superseded his desire to run his own business. Given this scenario, how could Richard lower his stress level?

The first step in solving this problem was for Richard to make a realistic appraisal of his actual skills, competence, and emotional needs. After this evaluation, Richard had to explore the following possibilities: the acquisition of further skills to build up his confidence to an effective functioning level; the return to a practice with other osteopaths who would lend him the professional and emotional support he needed; or a career change. Richard had to decide how he wished to proceed.

If Richard had been aware of his own limitations and the reality of the advantages and disadvantages of being a solo practitioner, he would have thought twice about leaving a group practice. His history showed that he had very little trust in himself. He was not a particularly good student in public school, nor did he excel in medical school. He entered the osteopathic profession after he had been a successful personal trainer. While he enjoyed doing that work, he felt he was not in a highly prestigious profession. Therefore, Richard decided to upgrade his level of skills and become an osteopath. In this way, he could give greater help to people and, at the same time, feel more important and admired.

When he was faced with the isolation that attended a solo practice, he did not have enough basic confidence in his own competence to deal with the stress of that change. Being involved with needy patients made this change hard to tolerate as he, himself, was needy.

The daily challenges that he found difficult to meet were eroding his already low self-esteem. His self-perceived inadequacy which, unfortunately, was real, further cut into his confidence level and created physical and emotional problems that kept him from functioning effectively. Because his stress level was so high, he couldn't think clearly about how to solve this problem. Instead he felt locked in, trapped, and unable to escape.

When Richard became aware of what had happened to him and began to accept and appreciate his own strengths and weaknesses, he decided to close his solo practice and return to his first love — personal training. As he put his life back together, his anxieties subsided and he was able to function productively once again.

APPLICATION

To clarify your own inner and outer faces of stress, are you able to look at yourself as objectively as possible when you are faced with new tasks and/or changes in your life? Before you risk, it is important to find out if you have the skills and the emotional and physical strength that the changes will demand. You can discover this by an objective appraisal of yourself, based on your performance history and an understanding of your inner face of stress, as well as a realistic evaluation of the outer face of stress. The following "project plans" will help you become aware of your own strengths and weaknesses in the two faces of stress.

BLUEPRINT #1

THE IMPACT OF STRESS ON PRODUCTIVITY

INDIVIDUAL PROJECT PLANS

1. Describe your own inner face of stressby answering the following questions:

    How do you respond to a change, either "good" or "bad"?

    To being corrected?

    To being challenged?

    To being promoted?

    To being passed over for a promotion?

    Give examples to go along with your descriptions so you are sure you have evaluated yourself correctly.

2. Describe your outer face of stress by answering the following questions:

    Is your work environment tense and demanding?

    Do you have tight schedules to meet, or is the time frame rather flexible?

    Do you have supportive relationships at work?

    Are you enjoying yourself at home and at work? If not, why not? What are some of the stressors preventing you from doing so?

    How long a commute do you have every day? Is it in a highly congested area?

3.   Do you feel competent and confident in your job? If not, what can you do to improve your skills to raise your level of competence?

4.   What are some of your behaviors or feelings at home and at work? Use the following questions as a guide:

Are you smoking more? Drinking more?

Sleeping badly?

Eating poorly?

Exercising enough?

Do you find it difficult to concentrate?

Are you getting less pleasure out of life because you are preoccupied?

Are you less tolerant of your friends and colleagues?

Do you have a loving and supportive relationship with someone? Do you give ample time to nurturing this relationship?

Do you always seem to be in a rush?

When you are driving in traffic, are you relaxed and willing to flow with what is out there, or are you uptight, blowing your horn, cussing the other drivers, and weaving in and out of traffic?

5.   If your answers indicate a high degree of stress, try to figure out what the triggers are that are causing these symptoms. Write them down.

6.   What kind of home do you live in? Structured or laissez-faire? How does this impact your work performance?

7.   Do you feel your inner face and outer face of stress are in harmony? If not, why not, and what can you do to improve the balance between them?

8.   On a scale of 1 to 10, 1 being the lowest and 10 the highest, rate your average daily stress level over a two week period.

9.   Study your "stress graph" and decide in which areas of your life you need to make changes.

BLUEPRINT #1

THE IMPACT OF STRESS ON PRODUCTIVITY

COMPANY PROJECT PLANS

1.   Describe your company environment. Is it a highly stressed one or not?

2.   If it is a tense environment, what can you do to help change it into a more comfortable place? Be specific.

PROJECT PLAN NOTES

INTERACTIONS AND STRESS

In this blueprint, we are concerned with the third face of stress: the interpersonal one. All three faces, the inner, the outer, and the interpersonal, interact with one another to affect your stress level either positively or negatively. In Blueprint #1, you learned about the first two faces of stress. In understanding the third face, you will be able to put together a complete picture of how you handle your daily stressors.

THE THIRD FACE OF STRESS

The interpersonal face has to do with your relationships with others. How do you get along with those around you? at work? at home? How much stress does your boss give you? your employees? your colleagues? your customers? How do you deal with demanding people? with those who are different from you? your husband or wife? your children? your parents? your friends?

The way you relate to others has its origin in your early family life and your own personal sense of who you are. How were you reared? What did you see? What were your own experiences with others? Your past life and inner make-up contribute to your sense of self-esteem. High self-esteem lets you reach out to others, to be assertive, and feel comfortable doing so. You have a healthy sense of your own worth and are unafraid to express opinions, to be a friend to others, and to share your feelings. With high self-esteem, there is an ease about your interactions. As a result, others feel comfortable around you.

Low self-esteem feeds upon itself. If you are afraid to reach out to people, if you question yourself with regard to others, you will find it very difficult to be as effective as you could be. Your stress level will rise as you venture into areas of which you are uncertain. This anxiety, if too debilitating, will not allow you to change course easily. Therefore, your finding and taking opportunities to interact advantageously with others will be very difficult. And yet, if you do not change the way you relate, your feelings about yourself will continue their downward spiral unabated. Low self-esteem is a formidable barrier to productivity.

In Blueprint #1, you read about Richard, who was not only impacted by the inner and outer faces of stress but was also immersed in the third face, the interpersonal. Richard was in a profession that required high self-esteem, since he dealt with needy and vulnerable people. He had to give of himself in order to help them recover. His interaction with his clients had to be positive for him to be effective. Unfortunately, Richard's feelings of inadequacy prevented him from doing his job. When things were going well for Richard, he was able to reach out. As soon as he ran into difficulty, however, his low self-esteem got in the way, and he began to perceive a situation that was very threatening. His low energy level, a result of being depleted daily by his stressors, made it difficult for him to meet the requirements of his task. Thus, the interpersonal face of stress contributed more stress than he was already receiving from his inner and outer forces. This onslaught made it almost impossible for Richard to climb out of the abyss without getting some help.

How you interact with others is determined, to a great extent, by your feelings about yourself. When you are feeling irked by your fellow employees or your boss, or "used" by a friend, what do you do about it? Do you swallow the hurt and build your anxiety/stress level? Or do you confront it, in a healthy way, not an angry one? Do you listen to the other person? Or do you feel so uneasy that listening is difficult? Do you feel in command of yourself so that an effective interaction can occur? In other words, do you express your feelings in ways that give you a sense of being in control of the situation without threatening the other person?

Many times, when people confront a problem head-on, they do it with anger. Better to cool down and discover the other person's viewpoint, so that you G-R-O-W in the relationship as a result of new understanding and a connection with the other person.

How you handle yourself with others is a key to whether you build stress within yourself or diminish it. Your interpersonal relations can spell success in your family, in your social relations, and in your job.

CHOICES

In order to help diminish stress, you have to determine your choices. What choices do you have when you feel trapped as a husband, a wife, or an employee? Do you think you really have a choice to change something if someone's behavior is giving you difficulty? What can you change? Can you alter the other person, the situation, or yourself? In order to understand another point of view, it is necessary to understand yourself first. Knowing that you can only change yourself, which can ultimately lead to changing the situation, puts you in control. If you focus on changing the other person, you will feel powerless and impotent. Realistically, you cannot change anyone else.

When feeling powerless in an interpersonal situation, people are inclined to swallow the hurt. They appear unable to express an opinion that will be at odds with the other person. They feel helpless to question the other person's viewpoint. Feeling overwhelmed and trapped by their own inability to express themselves they begin to develop resentment toward the other person. While they do not thihnk they have any choice in this kind of interaction, in fact, they are making a choice, albeit an unconscious one. And that is to allow the other person to run roughshod over them!

BURYING YOUR FEELINGS

So many times when you bury your feelings, you begin to develop a list of hurts which can affect your health as well as your interpersonal relationships. When you bury your feelings, you also cover your eyes. You fail to see what is really happening out there because you are so focused on your own internal stress. When you are able to look, you can begin to understand the real problem and start to correct it.

How do you do that? The interpersonal face of stress deals with the problems created within a relationship. It occurs when two or more people come together with their own set of inner and outer stressors and attempt to communicate with one another. In order to go beyond your own feelings and try to understand the feelings of the other person, you first have to be able to listen to your own rhythms. You have to understand and deal with your own motivations, your own agenda, before you can begin to understand those of others. When you are able to look at yourself objectively, you are then able to put yourself in the other person's shoes. At this point, you can begin to effect changes in your style of relating to that person which, in time, should alter the interaction.

THE OTHER PERSON

What are the motivations for his behavior? Would this person really set out to hurt you, or is he simply trying to get the job done in the most expedient way possible? How do you know this? How do you get to the heart of the issue?

By questioning the motivation of the particular *behavior*, you will have the key to the lock of being interpersonally effective. You must concentrate on the behavior and not on the person. What did he do? By focusing on the behavior you do not attack the person. By confronting the issue, not the person, you can begin to change the situation. You may think the other person is a dummy, but don't say it!

If this is still difficult for you, then there is another way of handling the problem. By talking to someone else, an uninvolved and trusted third party, you get another perspective and increased understanding.

Do you know someone you can trust with your feelings and your thoughts? Is there someone in your life with whom you feel safe in letting your hair down? Or do you think it is a sign of weakness to tell somebody what you are really thinking and feeling? How you respond to these questions will give you insight into your inner face of stress as well as your interpersonal one.

These are the aspects of yourself that you bring to your relationships. In order to implement more effective ways of relating to others, you have to understand and be aware of your own inner face of stress. By using the Project Plans in Blueprint #1, you will become more knowledgeable about some of the factors that may be affecting your interpersonal relations.

Everyone has his or her own tolerance level for stress. It can be likened to the load a table can carry. Each table, because of the kind of wood used and the method of construction, can hold a certain amount of weight. Even though two tables may look alike, their load levels are different. And so it is with people. Each one of us has a different tolerance for stress because of our genetic makeup and the environmental factors that shaped us.

The following illustration puts together the three faces of stress: the inner, outer and interpersonal. As managers, in order to help yourself and your company become more productive, you have to know the triggers that cause stress to turn into distress in you and in others. Like the table, everyone is unique. With this in mind, you need to be aware of how large a load you and your staff can carry. In this way, you will be able to surmount the barriers to personal and company productivity.

ILLUSTRATION

I was consulting for a small business (about 50 people) that was having great difficulty in many areas. Bill, the Managing Director and owner, was in complete charge of the company. He was not a skillful manager and did not enjoy this position. As a result, he was not having much success in running the business. Some of the problems he had were in sales, production, delivery scheduling, and inventory control.

In order to make the business more efficient, Bill decided to hire a plant manager to run the company on a daily, hands-on basis. While Bill would remain as Managing Director, he would function in the background, giving the plant manager carte blanche to run the company. Bill chose John, an older man with little executive experience, as the plant manager. His functions were clear and specific. Bill promised John a bonus if he could meet his objectives and if the company profit margin were to reach a certain point. John, having been out of work for a long time and eager for a job, decided to accept the offer and take on the role of plant manager. Without a written contract, John accepted the terms of the agreement and was told to be ready to discuss the situation in a few months.

As soon as John took over, he proved to be an aggressive and autocratic boss, inclined to attack problems head-on without discussion with his staff. He was determined to reverse the course of the company single-handedly. He arrived at work at 6 a.m. and went home past 8 p.m. He was a tough taskmaster, for himself as well for others. Saturdays and Sundays he called in people to expedite orders. To meet special requests, he felt it was necessary to break production schedules.

John appeared to be everywhere: manufacturing, marketing, shipping. He was giving orders rather than listening. It appeared that he valued only his own input He was on the telephone with new business and involved with trying to get a government grant. In the wake of all this frenetic activity, he was creating ill will among the staff. Was anyone overseeing this man? Where was Bill, his boss?

Bill decided to take a back seat during all this. He didn't involve himself with the operational end of the business. One of the reasons he hired a plant manager was that he, the Managing Director, didn't want to have anything to do with the day-to-day operations of the plant. He realized he was not very successful in that capacity and was far more comfortable functioning in the role of the creative genius behind the business. He wanted to devote himself to dreaming up new products. Thus John, the plant manager, became the key individual in the operation of this company and was allowed full rein to do whatever he wanted, and in the way he wanted, in order to meet his objectives. No one was overseeing him or interacting with the employees to get their reaction to the change in leadership.

After John had been on the job for several months, he finally asked Bill to discuss the terms of his agreement so that they could draw up a formal contract. At this time, promises made were not kept. As a result, John lost his cool, became highly emotional, and broke down. It was at this point that

Bill called me in as a consultant. The theme of our meeting was how unacceptable the plant manager's behavior was during their last meeting together!

WHAT'S GOING ON?

Obviously, there were several factors at work here. John's stress level was being tested constantly as he tried, all by himself, to turn the company around. Not only did he not involve anyone else in decision-making, but because of Bill's aloofness and apparent disinterest in the day-to-day operations of the company, John operated as a Lone Ranger. He did not attempt to bring the disparate and dysfunctional elements of the company together. While Bill decided to take a back seat and give John the freedom to do whatever he thought was necessary to get this plant running efficiently, he took too much of a back seat. He gave neither advice, suggestions, encouragement, or support. Bill, in effect, was guilty of abdication, not delegation. And when the time came to review what had been happening and write a formal contract, he focused on John's behavior during the meeting. That was the trigger that caused Bill to call me in for help. He could not understand how a man could become so emotional! He never saw his own culpability in John's breakdown. By failing to respect another man's tolerance for stress, not only during the meeting but through the many months when John was driving himself and the staff to distraction, he did not act responsibly or intelligently.

John could have avoided the breaking down of his emotions had he been in touch with his own inner face of stress to determine how much he could tolerate. He also needed to be aware of the outer face of stress, the actual condition of this company and how much change the employees could tolerate. Had he analyzed the situation realistically, he would have realized he could not turn this company around without the support of Bill and his staff. He also would have known that he could not work the many hours he did and become personally involved in every facet of the business without its taking its toll on himself as well as the staff. Not only was it very bad physically and emotionally for John and everyone in the company, it was exceedingly bad management. How long the employees were going to put up with this was yet another question. John's effectiveness was constantly being eroded by the interpersonal face of stress as he failed to form quality relationships within the company.

SOLUTIONS

What would have been an effective management style with the objective of building interpersonal relationships and lowering the stress level within this company? In the beginning, John, as plant manager, should have looked more and acted less. He should have listened more and talked less. Had he been an effective manager, he would have invested his time wisely by getting to know the people who knew the company. He would have involved his people in strategic decision-making and delegated responsibly. (See Blueprint #9) With the effective use of the people who knew the business well, John could have concentrated on rebuilding the infrastructure. By enlisting their support, he would have begun building a team of capable, involved, and responsible employees. In doing this, he would have built interpersonal relationships which would have contributed to the productivity of this company and, perhaps, reversed the direction in which it was going. His management style was destroying, not building, relationships. While he may have made some profit in the short run, the long-term prognosis for this company was not a good one.

Bill, the Managing Director, by ignoring what was going on, removed himself from all responsibility and contributed to the plant manager's undoing. Bill and John were both primarily interested in the short-term reward, losing sight of the long-term gain which was required for the company to be a solid business entity. This could be accomplished only by having a workable strategy and capable people involved in the daily running of the business.

Bill was also guilty of ignoring the motivating factors that caused John to work so compulsively, to the detriment of John's own health and that of his employees. The idea of a bonus, from both a monetary and emotional point of view, was a strong motivator for a man who had been out of work for a long time. John had accepted a low salary to do a very difficult job because he needed the money. He also needed to boost his flagging self-esteem with the personal satisfaction of knowing he could get the job done well.

By telling John that the profit margin really was not what it appeared to be, Bill came forth with a stick rather than the carrot he had promised. At this point, John's stress level reached the breaking point.

Bill finally asked John to resign. Ultimately, Bill, the Managing Director—like Humpty Dumpty—had a great fall as the company faced bankruptcy. Unfortunately, all the king's horses and all the king's men could not put Humpty Dumpty together again.

John's and Bill's inability to understand themselves and others contributed more than a little bit to the demise of this company. In the Project Plans section which follows this Blueprint, there are questions directly related to the above illustration which may help you find a direction in your own company that will help make it more cohesive and productive. As you begin to think about these factors, the implementation of your own job should become more effective and efficient.

Do employees have a responsibility in determining their level of effective functioning? Do they feel free to discuss with their supervisor solutions to problems that may allow stress levels to be reduced? Is the supervisor open to these discussions? Understanding and feeling understood go hand in hand, raising morale and lessening stress. As job satisfaction increases, excitement, involvement, stimulation— all healthy aspects of being alive—become the order of the day. As this occurs, individual productivity—which leads to company productivity—rises.

SUMMARY

In talking about the three faces of stress—the inner, outer, and interpersonal—companies, as well as individuals, must look at themselves and the demands they make. The people in charge: the executives, managers, and supervisors must be aware of the stressors, which rob both the employer and employee of realizing their potential. We have to remember that, like the table, we are all unique. And we need to be aware of and respect those individual differences in ourselves and others if we are going to be successful.

The key to the lock of stress and productivity is to be able to step back and analyze yourself and the situation in order to understand what is going on. You need to know what gives you that tight feeling in your stomach, that headache, that anxious feeling that makes it difficult to concentrate.

The solution to lowering stress and building productivity is to be able to face the issues and not ignore them. When you ignore them, you pile up stress like ammunition, which has a negative effect on productivity. And you can be sure that stockpile will explode eventually, just as it did for Richard, John and Bill. By standing back and analyzing what is happening to you, your colleagues, and your company, you will be able to determine the problem in order to arrive at a solution.

BLUEPRINT #2

INTERACTIONS AND STRESS

INDIVIDUAL PROJECT PLANS

On a scale of 1 to 10, 10 being the highest and 1 being the lowest, rate your stress level where indicated.

1.   How do you get along with those around you? at work? at home? Stress level in each category?

2.   How much stress does your boss give you? your employees? your fellow workers? your customers? your husband or wife? your children? your parents? your friends? Stress level in each category?

3.   How do you deal with demanding people? With those who are different from you? Be specific.

4.   How were you were reared? (Permissively? Strictly?) What were some of your experiences growing up that made you feel good about yourself? Did you have a trusted friend while growing up? Do you have one now? How would you rate your comfort level with other people? Stress level?

5.   Do you share your feelings easily? How do you get rid of pent-up emotions as a result of the interpersonal face of stress?

6.   Are you assertive or passive? How do you handle confrontations? Use the scale of 1 to 10 to rate yourself, 1 being the least effective, and 10 the most effective.

7.   How well do you listen? Ask someone else to rate you on the scale of 1 to 10.

BLUEPRINT #2

INTERACTIONS AND STRESS

COMPANY PROJECT PLANS

1.   Is there anything in the illustration reminiscent of your present company? If so, what has to be changed? How would you change it?

2.   Is it the responsibility of the person in charge to understand how far and how much an employee can be pushed? Do you know of a recent example?

3.   What is the manager's role in keeping harmony in a business or department?

4.   Do you feel free to discuss problems with your supervisor?

5.   Do your employees trust you and feel free to discuss problems with you? Have your employees rate the trust level in your department.

6.   In the Illustration, what was the managing director's major error? What was the plant manager's major error?

7.   How do you determine whether there are problems within your department? What do you do in order to solve them?

PROJECT PLAN NOTES

PROJECT PLAN NOTES

WHY BUSINESSES FAIL

On the topic of U. S. business failures, John Silber, then president of Boston University, stated that one of the reasons that many U. S. businesses lose a share of the market to foreign competitors is short-sighted corporate management, which emphasizes quarterly profits over long-term improvements.

The short-term profit motive usually motivates the people in charge not to invest enough money to keep the business current, thereby ignoring technological changes within their bailiwick. Being focused on the short term, they also may tend to ignore the competition within their industry, the economic environment, and the interconnectedness of the world.

Underlying all these factors, however, are the "soft skills," which are often overlooked as the foundation which keeps the infrastructure strong. Many times, businesses do not put enough money, energy and time into training programs which focus on employer/employee relations, management skills, and interpersonal relations inside the company, as well as with distributors, suppliers, and customers. These programs should involve every member of the organization, from the company president to the receptionist, and in that order.

Business failures can occur when the individuals in charge, satisfied with the status quo, do not invest in their employees. They believe that what is happening today will be there tomorrow. As long as the profit margin remains within their projections, they are convinced that the business is doing well, and is going to continue to do well. These people are wearing blinders.

Reluctance to invest both in upgrading technological aspects of the business and in honing the "people skills" indicates a lack of understanding of the challenge of business. Both elements are essential to a successful organization.

Businesses are people. The more open they are to change and progress, the more astute and aware they will become, and vice versa. The more willing they are to meet the challenge of change, the greater the chance of business success. The successful business person knows that the status quo is very fleeting. Status quo is based on the past; it has nothing to do with anticipation of and preparation for the future. Successful people are never satisfied with the status quo.

IMPORTANCE OF PEOPLE

To have successful companies, management must value their employees. Companies change, either positively or negatively, for a variety of factors, not the least of which emanates from the way employees feel about themselves in relation to the company.

One of the most significant factors in any organization's success is the way people are treated by management, and how the employees perceive they are being treated. Is management sending the right message? This is an area that requires a great deal of time and effort on the part of management. It needs to be looked at as an investment in productivity, and not as time lost.

One of the most damaging organizational stressors occurs when employees feel they have no input into the business, when they feel that management is unresponsive to their ideas and feelings. Nothing seems to bother people more than believing they are being ignored. And nothing will destroy productivity faster than an employee who feels management is unaware of her presence.

THE SUPERVISORY ROLE

How can you avoid the loss of productivity because of unmotivated employees? Supervisors are seen as emissaries of management. They have to know what to filter down and what to filter up. Even though today the hierarchy has been flattened to a great extent because of teams and consensual management, supervisors, in some form, will always be around. What does the employee need to know in order to feel a vital part of the team? And what does management need to be apprised of in order to understand the needs of the employee and the business?

As a supervisor, you must know your employees and how they function. You must be aware of how they respond to the demands of the business, and what their strengths and weaknesses are. You need to be open to their perceptions and opinions. Do they have input into decision making? Are they given a chance to suggest ways to improve productivity? All this goes beyond knowing only the content part of their job, or yours. You have to ask questions which tap into their knowledge of the job and the company. You have to listen to the answers to these questions. Then you need to be responsive, so that the employee feels significant. This type of relationship contributes to employees feeling important, visible, and valued. This type of relationship promotes productivity as it enhances morale. All of this requires a significant investment of time, effort, and organization. It cannot be a casual exercise in off-the-cuff meetings by happenstance.

Another factor in productivity is how much you enjoy your co-workers. Is there camaraderie in the group? Cooperation? Spirit? Trust? Do you enjoy working together?

In any organization, there will be conflicts among people. Many times, employees bring their own personal stressors to the job, which can cause friction among their co-workers. A department, like an orchestra, is as strong as its weakest player. All day long, you have interactions with people you like, some you don't like. You must accommodate, confront, compromise, agree, disagree, accept, tolerate, and enjoy. These kinds of interactions can produce stress, which can rob you of your productivity.

If you have a team, and there is one person on that team who is negatively affecting morale and productivity, it is your responsibility to find out the reasons why. Are there personal stressors involved? Are there environmental stressors? Which face, or faces, of stress are you dealing with? You must be able to help that individual change, or you and he will have to deal with the consequences of not changing. There is nothing more demoralizing in a company than having people around who cannot, or will not, adapt to the company culture.

These factors all deal with interactions among people as well as the impact of the environment. They have to do with the second and third faces of stress, the outer face and the interpersonal face.

There are many factors that contribute to the success or failure of a business. The short-sighted view of management fails to recognize the significance of change, not only in technology but in its staff. No matter how good the product, management must invest in the people. Interpersonal relationships can have a profound impact on the success or failure of a company.

BLUEPRINT #3

WHY BUSINESSES FAIL

INDIVIDUAL PROJECT PLANS

1.   Do you enjoy your job? Why? Is it money? Is it status? Do you feel involved and significant in the running of your company?

2.   Do you enjoy being with the people in your department? Is there camaraderie? Is there loyalty toward the company and trust in each other's ability to do the work required?

3.   Write a brief description of yourself: your strengths, your weaknesses, your goals, and your contribution to your company.

4.   Rate yourself as to your effectiveness on the job: 10 being the highest, and 1 the lowest. Rate your company on its responsiveness to suggestions: 10 being the highest and 1 the lowest.

BLUEPRINT #3

WHY BUSINESSES FAIL

COMPANY PROJECT PLANS

1.   Does the company encourage employee involvement in decision making?

2.   How do you, as a manager, promote a sense of trust in and loyalty toward the company?

3.   If you are a supervisor, write down the name of each member of your department and what you know about him or her. What motivates each one? Is every member contributing to the benefit of the department? What are each one's strengths and weaknesses?

4.   Do all members of your department feel important to the company? If so, why? What is it your company does that promotes this kind of feeling? If not, why not? What needs to be done to promote this kind of feeling?

5.   Are your employees encouraged to suggest ways to improve productivity?

6.   How do you show your employees that you value them and their contribution to the company?

7.   How do you get feedback from your employees?

8.   Rate your company on its responsiveness to suggestions from your employees: 10 being the highest and 1 the lowest.

PROJECT PLAN NOTES

PROJECT PLAN NOTES

PEOPLE AS ASSETS AND COSTS

"An organization has to treat people as assets... they require valuing, investing, respect...and they will respond with quality output and increased productivity as they feel cared about and valued. If you look upon people as costs...you will behave very differently toward them and, as a result, you will get very different responses (negative, uncaring, lack of quality, no identification with the company, lack of loyalty, etc.)"

–Handy

I believe this philosophy to be the foundation of every successful organization. Companies are people. In running companies, people need to be driven by some concept or thinking that gives them a road map on how to behave. This road map has been called the "mission" of a company. It is, in fact, the underlying premise on which a company is based and determines the culture of the organization.

In many Blueprints, I discuss valuing and caring. I believe this theme must be the guiding force within every organization. The above quotation puts those qualities in a new light: assets vs. costs. You cannot look at people only as costs if you want your company to run smoothly. *People* make the company move, not costs.

For the very reasons listed in Handy's statement, people respond differently if they are viewed as assets. From this viewpoint, they are treated as significant, important, and meaningful. That's when they begin to take ownership of their work, as they feel what they do is being appreciated. They take responsibility if they feel listened to and not talked at. They know what's going on because they are told the WHY of decisions. They are asked for their opinions and given credit for being able to think and solve problems. And they are not overworked.

Being overworked is a big problem in companies today, as staffs are thin. Companies are called leaner and meaner. Unfortunately, the two usually go together. And that is one reason why morale is low and productivity is not as high as companies would like. Morale and productivity go hand in hand. Overworked people are resentful and tired. Their potential is not being tapped. They are unhappy and fatigued. They are also frightened of losing their jobs, so that anxiety may haunt them as they go through the day. Anxiety, or fear, reduces productivity.

ILLUSTRATION #1

I had occasion to meet with a young woman who happened to be a specialist in a school system. Mary's job consisted of going from school to school, rendering her services to those children who were referred to her for special help. Since she was the only one able to give this help, her roster of clients was quite large. She knew that the current setup was not serving herself, her clients, or the system, and she tried to communicate this to the administration.

She was caught, however, in an organization that was unyielding in its demands. She was allowed exactly forty minutes per session to teach a group of fifteen students ranging in age from six to twelve with a wide variety of problems. Since each of these children had different needs and different abilities, based on age, grade level and developmental stage, Mary had to group them. She was frustrated at the lack of time she had to devote to each child who needed more attention than she was able to give within this setting.

Mary complained to the administration countless times about the time allowance, which was too short, and the number of children in each group, which was too large. She also told them she could not accommodate the many children that needed her services; she was only one person and could not stretch herself any farther. She made it clear that the children's needs were not being met because of the constraints of the system.

All this brought her into my office, suffering from stress induced by her own desire to do a good job, and her apparent inability to perform well, given the conditions under which she worked.

WHAT TO DO?

The question was, what could Mary do to solve this problem so that her stress level would go down and her productivity go up? What did she have to do to feel good about her performance?

First, she had to understand the underlying philosophy of this company—the school system. It did not look at people as assets but rather as costs. This viewpoint obviously encompassed the children as well as the teachers. So how could she change the situation? Should she sit back, accept it, and feel unrewarded and depressed at the end of the day? Should she go through the motions, accepting very little progress as the results of her labor? How could she tap into her own potential and the potential of her students, given the underlying philosophy of the organization in which she worked?

Unfortunately, when people are caught in such a company, they lose their desire to try to solve their problems. They see their task as daunting and the problems as insurmountable. This attitude, of course, leads to the behavior that Handy talks about in the opening quotation: "negative, uncaring, lack of quality, no identification with the company, lack of loyalty, etc." You can see the results of the performance meted out by people with this attitude. Fortunately, Mary hadn't reached this level of apathy, so she could still deal with changing her behavior despite rather grim odds.

SOLUTIONS

Once Mary became aware of the company's philosophy, she had to come up with solutions that could serve the children, herself, and the system. If she understood the company's basic philosophy, she might be able to show them in dollars and cents how she could benefit them if they would make specific changes. She needed to outline these changes. Obviously, people were not important here, just costs.

Was this a realistic response to Mary's problems? According to Mary, it was not. She claimed the company was not interested in her solutions. From her experience, she believed they expected her to work within the bounds set by the administration.

If this was true, then Mary needed to go further and ask herself whom she was serving. Was it the system or the children? And who was responsible for the children?

When you analyze it this way, the answer becomes clear. The parents were the ones who had leverage within this system. And it was the parents who had to take responsibility for seeing that their children's needs were being met.

While Mary could not appear to be rebellious and working against authority, she had to devise a way to get her message across to the parents without undermining the system or her job. She also could not risk being seen by the administration as a "complainer", but rather had to be seen as an involved, loyal and conscientious employee. In addition, she could not appear to be inadequate in her skills, and thus the cause of the children not learning in her class. Therefore, she needed to devise some sort of solution to optimize the performance of the students and not jeopardize her standing in the system.

An easy task? Far from it. But in setting about to implement a solution, she was going to energize herself and diminish her high anxiety level, which was affecting her sleep, appetite, and performance. If she couldn't accomplish this, she either had to settle for mediocrity or find another venue for her services.

OPTIONS

One of the problems with being treated as a cost is that people feel trapped. They don't see themselves as having any choice, other than to continue in the same demoralizing way day after day. The key to the lock of productivity is to know you have options, and to set about finding them and implementing them one at a time in order to seek a solution. In all fairness, working in a company that values people as costs rather than assets can be a harrowing experience. But once you are aware of and understand that, you can begin to change things for yourself. There is no point in fighting the system. All you will do is suffer what my young client did before she sought help: feel battered, bruised, and frustrated. And in the middle of such turmoil, you will not be one step closer to solution.

ILLUSTRATION #2

Rob was a young man who came to me in a stew about a decision he had to make which was driving him to distraction. He was a single man about thirty-two years old who wanted to buy a house. He had found one he considered ideal and had put a deposit on it. Although the house was quite affordable given his means, he hadn't slept well or been able to enjoy himself since he had made his decision. The "what-ifs" were getting to him.

In order to calm him down, we went over his finances and projected possible costs. When all was reviewed, he was assured he was able to afford his payments, given the size and length of his mortgage. So what was his problem?

It seems that Rob's major concern was about his job. Unfortunately, he worked in a company which viewed people as costs rather than assets. As a result, Rob was in constant fear of being outplaced. He worried about his performance and found himself working long hours in order to get his work done and not create any waves. Whenever anyone asked him to do something, whether it was appropriate or not, Rob would do it. He never took any time off or asked for any favors. In fact, he had planned a bike trip and needed to leave work one hour early on the Friday of the projected trip. Rob was not going to ask for this time because he was afraid that he would be seen as not doing his job. He was willing to forego the first night of his trip (a two-day trip, by the way, which would have been cut in half by his unwillingness to ask for an hour off!) rather than be viewed as a shirker.

When the time came for him to make a decision on his house, he panicked. Although he had reviewed the numbers over and over again, he was still very anxious about the projected purchase. Everything seemed to converge on him all at once and he felt overwhelmed. He couldn't see the proverbial forest for the trees. In light of the house purchase, he was planning to cancel his fitness center enrollment, which he needed for social as well as physical reasons. In fact, Rob was willing to deny himself pleasure because he was locked up in fear over his job and his perceived possibility of not being able to manage his debts in the event of job loss.

Rob and I had to discuss what *he* valued. How did he see himself? Did he value himself in such a way that he felt important and worthwhile? Did he feel competent and confident in his skills? If so, why was he acting the way he did? What was going on at work? Was he doing a good job? Could he, in fact, lose his job if he asked for one hour off? As for his house, why couldn't he see this acquisition as a long-term project and still continue to have fun in his life while he lived in a new and pleasant environment? Did *he* view himself as an asset or a cost? Did he treat himself with love and respect? Did he think he deserved to be treated fairly? Why would he pay for a bike trip and then give up one day out of two so as not to ask for one hour off? What was going on?

SENSE OF PERSPECTIVE

It's obvious from these two illustrations that bright, conscientious people who work in a system governed by the view of people as costs rather than assets can lose their way. They can become so fearful that their judgment gets skewed and their behavior becomes erratic, both on the job and in their personal life. This is not the way for companies to tap into the potential of their employees. In fact, just the opposite happens. People become so anxious that they are afraid to take risks, are less than creative, and soon find themselves lost in a system in which they feel trapped. Their personal lives are severely affected as their fear at work is transferred to their everyday living. In other words, they lose their sense of perspective and find themselves going through life with very little enjoyment either personally or professionally. They are bound up in fear and are afraid to do anything that will rock the boat.

In order to rectify this situation, they have to set about treating themselves as assets, valuing themselves so that they feel worthwhile. Otherwise, they are apt to make incorrect and unwise decisions. They have to step back from the situation, analyze the problem and begin to find solutions. The more options they can come up with, the less trapped they will feel. For this, they have to dig into their own value system and find out what it is they want out of life. And once they begin this search, they must invest in themselves in ways that will lead to the achievement of their goals.

BLUEPRINT #4

ASSETS
AND
COSTS

INDIVIDUAL PROJECT PLANS

1.   Do you view yourself as a cost or an asset?

2.   How is this view manifested in your daily life?

3.   Can you define your value system? Goals and objectives?

4.   Can you relate either to Mary or Rob in the above? How would you act in either instance?

5.   Put yourself in Rob's shoes: what are some of the possible ways for him to lower his anxiety level?

6.   Put yourself in Mary's shoes: how would you solve her problem?

BLUEPRINT #4

ASSETS AND COSTS

COMPANY PROJECT PLANS

1.   Does your company view people as costs or assets?

2.   Back up your answer with specific examples.

3.   How do you contribute to your company's philosophy?

PROJECT PLAN NOTES

BLUEPRINT #5

SELF-ESTEEM: A FACTOR IN PRODUCTIVITY

In an issue of *INC* magazine, there is a quote from Robert Darbin, who was founder, president, and chief executive officer of Scandinavian Design, Inc.

"There is only one thing that counts in business: building the self-esteem of your employees. Nothing else matters, because what they feel about themselves is what they give to your customers. If an employee comes to work not liking his job, not feeling good about himself, you can be sure that your customers will go away not liking or feeling good about your company."

Since companies are essentially people, it is reasonable to assume that if employees feel good about themselves and their job with the company, then they are going to represent that company in a positive light.

Self-esteem is the outgrowth of understanding, acknowledging, and appreciating the employee as an integral part of the business. How, then, does a company translate this into workable behaviors?

IMPLEMENTATION

How do you build the self-esteem of your employees? Can this be looked upon as a goal in supervising people? Or, perhaps, it is a "co-goal" — one that accompanies the achievement of the business objectives of which each employee should be aware. In achieving the agreed-upon goals, the employee, if given her due, should certainly experience a lift in self-esteem. Isn't this the way to make employees feel part of the company? If employees don't feel this way, can they be motivated to perform well? And isn't employee performance what we're talking about when we speak of "productivity"?

So how do supervisors motivate their staff to perform? Does the motivation to do a good job and represent the company in a good light emanate from self-esteem?

INTRINSIC vs. EXTRINSIC MOTIVATION

Intrinsically-motivated people do a particular task for the pleasure of the task itself. Extrinsically-motivated people are turned on primarily for reasons outside the self, such as pay, promotion, evaluation, prestige, or status. However, appropriate extrinsic rewards contribute to intrinsic motivation over time.

Extrinsic motivation is as necessary as intrinsic motivation. Too much focus either way is undesirable; there has to be a balance between the two. If too much emphasis is put on extrinsic motivation, it will be a deterrent to creativity in the long run. Supervisors have to understand this concept in order to motivate their staff.

JOB APPRAISAL

By scheduling regular appraisal sessions with your staff, you give yourself a chance to listen and learn, as well as to define your own criteria of job performance. This type of meeting gives the employee a chance to vent some of his frustrations and, if the supervisor is responsive, to come away knowing that the supervisor will attempt to implement solutions to many of the problems being voiced. This will contribute to the employee's feeling that he is important and valuable to the company. This type of interaction will also build trust and loyalty between the supervisor and her direct reports.

As an effective supervisor, you acknowledge what your staff is doing by seeing the positive aspects of an employee's performance first, and then correcting the aspects whose improvement could contribute to a better overall performance. If an employee feels valued (and there are many ways to value an employee beyond money and promotion, although these are important) the employee will contribute in many positive ways to the growth of your company. It all begins with the CEO and works its way down the line. The message comes from the top.

INCENTIVES

The need for all employees to be recognized as doing a good job contributes to their sense of self-esteem and their sense of loyalty toward and identification with the company. These are the ingredients that make soundly-run and well-functioning companies. This is what is meant by extrinsic motivation, and it goes beyond product and the mechanics of the job. It is something on which too few companies spend time and money, although people are the core of every business.

In another issue of *INC*, in an article called "Incentives That Don't Work" Bonnie Donovan of the American Productivity Center has this to say:

"To improve productivity, you have to foster teamwork, and singling out the superstars tends to undermine team spirit. If you really want to improve performance, then the rewards have to go to anyone who attains a given level of performance, and that level should be within reach of a lot of people."

With regard to boosting productivity by handing out recognition awards, Donovan further states:

"Most people don't know what they have to do to receive the recognition award. You've set up a target that nobody knows how to aim at."

Recognition awards can be very helpful if they are fair, and if the criteria for these awards are specifically and clearly spelled out and within reach of all. However, a recognition award in which one person is cited can affect morale negatively and be a turn-off for the rest of the department, team, or company.

47

If teamwork improves productivity, then why would you single out one person? A better way would be to give a particular award to the team or department that achieves the company's benchmarks of excellence. The award would have to consist of some form of recognition that is desirable to the people in that department. If you decide to give a bottle of wine to everyone on the team who does well, and one person is a teetotaler, the wine is not a motivator to higher productivity. The company has to come up with an award that is meaningful to all the people on the team.

By stressing a team recognition award, you are promoting involvement and cooperation. This is what every company has to strive for. By giving an award, you are recognizing good performance, which is healthy, appropriate, and self-esteem building.

PROBLEMS

Extrinsic motivation is needed, but it has to be balanced with intrinsic motivation—being motivated from within—which is the primary motivator in the final analysis. All members of a department or team would have to be utilizing resources, which will allow them to accomplish their goals. In other words, their strengths, not their weaknesses, would have to be employed. This is the route to esteem building and requires effective supervision and understanding of the kind of people that make up the team. Do they have the resources, individually and collectively, to contribute to the departmental goals? If not, the team will be sabotaged by anyone who is not intrinsically motivated to achieve. The need of supervisors to understand the people who report to them is absolutely vital in building a cohesive department, one which utilizes individual resources and works together toward the achievement of a common goal.

MORE INCENTIVES TO PRODUCTIVITY

An article in the *Wall Street Journal* suggested extending incentive pay deeper to lower management and key workers.

"Companies are offering more individual bonuses for performance gains to supervisors below top management and to engineers, investment officials

and others who they find aid the company. John Hancock Mutual Life Insurance rewards lower managers with up to ten per cent of their salary for 'extraordinary work.' ... Hewlett Packard Company gives two hundred to three hundred special stock options a year to employees who show extra accomplishment. Of seven hundred forty-seven employers polled by management consultant Hay Group, forty-nine per cent are offering individual incentives to lower managers; forty-eight per cent offer them to key professional and technical employees. Both figures are more than double a year ago."

Energy equipment maker Camco shuns such plans.

"We're pretty much team oriented, and we are not looking for a superstar."

So there are many schools of thought for you to ponder. There is no right answer. You must find what works best for you and your company.

ILLUSTRATION

I had occasion to redecorate my office and I decided to enlist the services of an office design company to help me. Susan, a very knowledgeable and pleasant woman, was assigned the task of drawing up plans and implementing them. I was extremely satisfied with her performance and felt it incumbent upon me to inform her manager of her outstanding job. I wrote a letter singing her praises and said that I hoped they would inform her of my feelings.

A few months later, I had to call Susan and, during the course of our conversation, I asked her if her supervisor had told her of my letter. I was stunned to hear that he had not. At that point, Susan began to pour out her frustrations about working in that company. While intrinsically motivated to do excellent work, Susan also thirsted for some extrinsic motivation in the form of praise, recognition, and greater compensation. She felt she was unappreciated, and my letter, which had gone unrecognized, only contributed to her feelings that she was being overlooked.

She also began to question the quality of her work. Was she as good as she thought she was, or was she fooling herself? I assured her that from my knowledge of her work, she was excellent at what she did. I told her not to let her employer's silence have power over her own judgment as to her capability. It seems they neither praised nor criticized her; they simply did not acknowledge anything she did.

A few months later, Susan called me to let me know that she had left her job and found employment elsewhere. She was working for less money but was extremely happy working for a "wonderful boss." What made him so "wonderful" was his appreciation of her work. He not only praised her but also asked her opinion on many of the projects being brought into the company. She felt that over the long term, she would do better financially and, very possibly, hold a significant position in the company.

SUMMARY
Thus, even with intrinsically-motivated people, supervisors must recognize employees in the form of praise, acknowledgment, ample pay, and promotional opportunities. All these contribute to the self-esteem of the employee, which goes a long way toward improving productivity.

BLUEPRINT #5

SELF-ESTEEM: A FACTOR IN PRODUCTIVITY

INDIVIDUAL PROJECT PLANS

1.   What kinds of incentives work best for you?

2.   Do you feel you are intrinsically motivated to do a good job for yourself and your company? If not, why not? What are the barriers standing in your way.

3.   Did you ever receive an employee recognition award? In what form? How did you feel about it? What was its impact on your motivation, in the short and long term? What impact did your award have on the motivation of the rest of the staff?

4.   Did you ever receive an employee award as part of a team effort? How did that affect your motivation and the motivation of your team in the short and long term?

5.   Does your immediate supervisor recognize your performance? How?

6.   On a scale of 1 to 10, 10 being the highest and 1 the lowest, rate your intrinsic motivation in your present job.

7.   On a scale of 1 to 10, 10 being the highest and 1 the lowest, rate your extrinsic motivation in your present job.

BLUEPRINT #5

SELF-ESTEEM: A FACTOR IN PRODUCTIVITY

COMPANY PROJECT PLANS

1.   What kinds of incentives do you think work best for your company?

2.   Look around your department and evaluate whether people are intrinsically motivated to do a good job for the company. What are some of the extrinsic motivators that have contributed, and continue to contribute, to their job performance?

3.   As a manager, what can you do to motivate your people to higher performance levels?

4.   Evaluate your job appraisal method. Is it effective? What can you do to make it more meaningful as defined in this Blueprint?

PROJECT PLAN NOTES

PROJECT PLAN NOTES

COMMUNICATION

Good communication is like a good
meal: nutritious, satisfying, and you
want to go back for more!

Why is good communication nutritious? Because it has all the essential ingredients for growth. An effective dialogue between two or more people should nourish the spirit the way food nourishes the body. Junk food simply fills the body for the moment. It has no nutritive value, so it doesn't promote healthy bodily growth. In fact, just the opposite can occur. Too much sugar or too much fat has a negative effect on the body and can cause problems if eaten over long periods of time.

Poor communication is similar to junk food. It simply does not promote good emotional or intellectual health. It can leave you feeling anxious and confused. It does not promote growth. Over a long period of time, poor communication can profoundly affect relationships, productivity, and personal well being.

SATISFYING

A good meal leaves a person with a tremendous sense of well-being. Pleasurable feelings accompany a good meal. The whole body responds emotionally as well as physically in harmony with the experience. The memory of a good meal gives joy for a long time as you relive it for its satisfying feelings.

Good conversation has a similar impact on the psyche and the emotions. You feel fulfilled and satisfied after the encounter. You have gained something. You feel understood. You do not feel alone. When you think about it, you feel fulfilled.

LET'S GO BACK FOR MORE

A good meal never leaves you feeling uncomfortable; it leaves you pleasantly satisfied. The taste and flavor stay in your memory so that you anticipate repeating the experience. Because of this, you return to the recipe or to the restaurant again and again. Each time you connect you are never let down. Each experience is as good as the last one.

So it is with a significant encounter. As you feel understood and in harmony, you also look forward to meeting with that person again. With each encounter you gain something. You do not dread the conversatio; you look forward to it. Whatever it was that passed between you has nourished each of you so that a relationship is being forged that will take you from one experience to another. No matter what the issue, you can count on that person not to let you down. The communication between you is honest, genuine, and caring. The reason it can remain open and honest is that you never feel judged or demeaned. Somehow the tone of the conversation is elevating and constructive. You feel nourished and satisfied each time you talk. You look forward to subsequent conversations, as you are never fearful of what may ensue.

MY BEST FRIEND

I wonder if all this is what people mean when they label someone their "best friend." Having a best friend implies that you have someone you can trust with your feelings, your most precious possession. You can feel certain that she will always be there for you and never violate your trust.

If you are fortunate enough to have a best friend, then, undoubtedly, you are someone else's best friend. If you know how to listen well (see Blueprint #7) and can communicate in the terms described above, then your friend, your spouse, or your children must feel that you are, indeed, their best friend.

YOUR COLLEAGUES

If you are an employer or supervisor, do you treat the people around you with the respect that good communication implies? If not, why not? Are the people who report to you your colleagues? Do they feel this way? Why or why not? How much easier and more fulfilling it would be for all of us if our conversation throughout the day were nourishing and satisfying as a tasty, nutritious meal!

If you have open and honest communication with those to whom you report, you can discuss your feelings and thoughts without fear of recrimination. Much of our anxiety comes from the third face of stress (see Blueprint # 2), having to do with interpersonal relations. Many people think that disagreement, or conflict, is unhealthy. What is unhealthy is the way they go about solving the problem. Some people feel tense, discounted, or diminished if someone has another opinion. Disagreements, or conflict, can make for healthy discussions and lead to healthy changes. How?

You have to know what it is you're disagreeing about. You have to stay away from personalities. You have to define the issues and stick with them. (See Blueprint #14) If you have healthy self-esteem, you will value what the other person is saying and welcome the input. You will not feel personally put down by conflict. If you find confrontation is a source of stress, try facing your next disagreement feeling the other person's opinion, as well as your own, is worthwhile. Concentrate on the problem and look for a solution to it. If this form of communication is carried off well, you will feel personally satisfied and fulfilled.

OTHER ASPECTS OF COMMUNICATION

One of the most important aspects of communication is its directness and honesty. How many times have you called someone and been told that she will call back...only never to hear from that person again? This call-back syndrome is code for "please don't bother me."

This type of communication can be very destructive. When it occurs, you don't know exactly what happened. Nothing is ever said directly. Promises were not kept, and you can't make contact to determine exactly what is going on. The motivation for this is usually a lack of courage (not time!) to confront the issue. What is the issue? Simply put, what is being offered is not wanted. Do you think it would be preferable to hear that directly, rather than to get the run-around and try to figure out the underlying message?

Let's take this symptom one step further and question whether this style could be part of the inner organization as well. If executives use this type of signal in dealing with an outsider, is it possible to conclude that they use the same style for people in their own organizations as well? (See Blueprint #14) Are signals being substituted for direct statements?

If so, credibility and approachability are being badly marred by a lack of directness. This style of communication creates a great deal of anxiety throughout an organization and has a negative impact on productivity. People will hesitate giving feedback if they know it will not be accepted. By putting up barriers to communication throughout an organization, a company is weakened. This type of communication models a form of behavior which, if operative, will lower morale and eventually lessen productivity.

OPEN DOOR POLICY

Many times, supervisors will tell me that they are always available to their employees. They have an "open door" policy. People can come in any time to discuss anything at all. The problem is, the supervisors complain, they can't get their work done because they are constantly being interrupted. I assure them that any feelings of animosity they have about this situation are perfectly in order. While having an "open door" policy may sound as if barriers have come down in the sphere of communication, in reality new ones are being erected. This policy is not sound practice in building productivity.

What does an open door policy mean? In the above instance, it meant, literally, the door was open all day long! Does this action contribute to the effectiveness of the staff if they know they can run to the supervisor for every little thing? And what effect does it have on the supervisor? What can be done to enhance communication and build productivity at the same time?

First, an open door policy does not have to mean "open all the time." It is advised that you post your hours of availability, e.g. 10-11 or 2-3, whenever you feel you want to take a break from your regular work to discuss problems with individual staff members "on demand." In this way, you promote three things:

Office structure. People know what to expect and learn to live within those bounds.

Independence. Staff members learn to become more independent as they try to figure out solutions, rather than wait to discuss the situation with the supervisor.

Greater productivity. It allows the supervisor to care about her own work load in a sensible way and still be open to her staff. It also promotes greater productivity among the staff as they learn to make decisions independently without putting matters on hold.

Obviously, this policy is only as good as the people implementing it. The supervisor has to be firm but friendly. He has to communicate his regrets when the hour is up and not make exception to this rule. During the open door hours, he should not accept telephone calls when in discussion with someone. After a while, people begin to accept this policy and understand its rationale.

A past issue of *USA TODAY* stated the following:

"Many offices are dens of festering feelings due to poor communication. Most situations don't get ironed out."

One of the reasons this happens is there are too many messages sent over the computers. This practice prevents face-to-face communication. Leaving your office and talking with someone directly is a way to break down barriers. In this way, you ask questions and get feedback from your boss, subordinates and peers as to what is going on. If you're not comfortable with interpersonal relationships other than on the computer, you will do yourself a favor to develop communication skills. Think about taking a course or just watching somebody who is a good communicator. Step back and figure out what that person does that is making him effective. Then, don't hide behind that computer. Go out and try it! Lines of communication must be open, from the top down, bottom to top, and laterally.

If this is done correctly, at the end of the day everyone will feel fulfilled, as if they have partaken of a very healthy meal: nutritious and satisfying. And tomorrow, they will be eager to go back for more!

BLUEPRINT #6

COMMUNICATION

INDIVIDUAL PROJECT PLANS

1.   Do you view your supervisor as your colleague? Do you trust her so that you can communicate openly with her?

2.   How do you feel about conflict? Disagreement?

3.   Do you feel free to express your opinion?

4.   Do you find yourself e-mailing everyone and not stepping out of your cubbyhole to talk directly with people?

BLUEPRINT #6

COMMUNICATION

COMPANY PROJECT PLANS

1.   Does your company culture encourage healthy communication? Define "healthy" as you understand it from the above Blueprint.

2.   If you are a supervisor, does your staff see you as someone they trust? How do you know?

3.   Do you view your staff as your colleagues?

4.   Ask your staff if they feel free to express their opinions. If they do not, what can you do to change this?

5.   On a scale of 1 to 10, with 1 being the lowest and 10 the highest, rate the communication in your company for openness, honesty, responsiveness. Ask your staff to do the same. What needs to be changed?

6.   Does your company encourage the use of interoffice memos, or does it look more kindly on face-to-face communication?

7.   What is your open door policy? Does it need repair?

PROJECT PLAN NOTES

PROJECT PLAN NOTES

COMMUNICATION INVENTORY

In order to inventory your communication skills, take an objective look at your interactions with your peers, your subordinates, your supervisor, and your family. Answer all the questions below to get an indication of how well you do in the communication department. And where you find you can't answer this yourself, please be sure to ask for feedback from someone you trust.

LISTENING IS THE HEART OF COMMUNICATION

No matter how many rules of communication there are, the one intrinsic factor in good communication is listening. How well do you listen?

What happens during your interactions with others, particularly with your peers, subordinates, and family? Do you do most of the talking? Or do you find yourself listening during the interchange? What are your feelings during the dialogue, and afterwards? Do you go away feeling you understand the other person's point of view? Could you repeat what you just heard? Or do you hear your own words repeating?

Do you feel the other person understands what you said? How do you know?

MORE THAN WORDS

Much besides words goes on during a conversation. There are things we do, the unspoken dialogue, that lets people know how we really feel. This other level gives rise to the thought: "What did he really mean?" The surrounding images, the body language, can enhance or destroy any interaction. The unspoken level can lead to feeling good after a dialogue and being motivated to do the work. Or, it can produce very negative feelings and contribute to anxiety or tension, which gets in the way of understanding and implementation.

What are some of your silent but powerful communicators that let a person know whether you consider him significant, important, worthwhile, or just plain equal?

SOME COMMUNICATORS

Do you look at the person you're talking with? Directly? Do you keep that eye contact while he's talking? Is the eye contact clear, so that the person knows you are truly listening? Or is the image one of preoccupation with your own thoughts, defenses, rebuttal, even while the other is speaking? The latter image can destroy any form of conversation, as a person feels he is not really being heard. And if you are thinking of your response, then he is probably correct in feeling that way.

If you're in your office and the telephone rings during a conversation, what do you do? Do you answer it, leaving the person with whom you were having the original conversation "hanging"? If that is the case, what is the message you're sending to that person in your office?

Are you always in a rush during a conversation, so that the person talking with you feels she has to talk so rapidly that she feels unfulfilled, unheard, unimportant, and anxious after the conversation?

When you make an appointment to see someone, are you on time? Do you give your undivided attention to the conversation?

If the conversation has to do with a project, at the end of the meeting do you ask the person to summarize the material covered, so that you can be sure you both understand what was said and what was heard?

Do you summarize what you have just heard, so that the person talking knows you have heard the message correctly?

Do you interrupt a lot?

Do you take the time to question, listen, and learn?

Do you listen to the answers?

Do you get back to people who are waiting for an answer from you or, if you consider it unimportant and not a high priority, do you just forget the conversation as soon as they leave?

Do you make promises you have no intention of keeping?

Do you take the time to recognize and reward effort, as well as results?

Do you take the time to confront issues and communicate tactfully but honestly about matters that do not please you?

Does information flow up and down in your organization with ease?

HOW TO CHANGE

If you try to maintain an objective distance during the next few days and just concentrate on one item at a time in the above inventory, you will be able to get a fairly accurate portrait of your communication strengths and weaknesses.

Communication is a skill that has to be developed. By taking your own pulse through this inventory, you will discover what you need to work on, and what your boss needs to work on as well. Don't be disturbed if you score rather low in the interaction department. Just set about working on your weaknesses, one at a time, and you'll be surprised how your own stress level, as well as the stress level in your department, will begin to go down. And your level of effective communication will rise proportionately!

BLUEPRINT #7

COMMUNICATION INVENTORY

INDIVIDUAL PROJECT PLANS

How well do you listen? Observe yourself in interactions throughout the day.

1.   Go over this inventory step-by-step and answer the questions posed.

2.   Ask your colleagues for feedback on your listening skills.

3.   Set goals for improvement.

PROJECT PLAN NOTES

CHANGING OURSELVES

Who said change is easy? It's one of the hardest things to come by. Why? Because no matter how difficult your situation is, you are used to it. Even if you are under a lot of stress, you will still resist changing the very things that are causing you frustration.

The other aspect of change that keeps many of us rooted in our old ways is the resistance and anxiety we meet from others as we attempt to change. And the answer, of course, is the same for the receiver as it is for the doer: everyone—including you—is used to your old ways. Change makes people uneasy.

Change also entails loss. Whether it is "good" change or "bad" change, there is loss involved. There are advantages and disadvantages to every form of change; thereby, you lose something as you gain something. Hopefully, the advantages outweigh the disadvantages, and that may make change easier.

And, yet, how is progress made unless we begin to look closely at ourselves, our companies, our lives, and determine what it is we can alter to promote greater productivity in every sphere?

The important thing to remember is that change is possible. Nothing is cast in cement. If we realize that we are doing things that are not rewarding or that are counterproductive, then isn't it possible that with this awareness, we can begin to make changes? That is the key to change: the awareness that something needs to be done to modify things. And it usually starts with you!

ILLUSTRATION

Anne was a first-level supervisor who was intent on being successful. She had twelve people reporting to her, and she thought she had things under control. However, her measure of control was to micro-manage and to be part of everything. Her anxiety level was high as she pushed her people to do more than they were capable of doing. Finally, one day, one of her direct reports lambasted her and threatened to quit. It was at this time that Anne called me. The episode created a great deal of anxiety in Anne. Suddenly, she was beginning to question her own adequacy as a supervisor.

What was happening to this very successful young woman? As we probed, she finally realized that she was putting all the burden on her people to change and was paying very little heed to her own behavior.

What were her expectations for this group? Was she becoming impatient with them? Was she aware of their strengths and weaknesses? How did she envision her role as supervisor? What was her behavior like? As she came under more and more stress, was she becoming irritable and angry with their apparent inability to fulfill her expectations?

AN OBJECTIVE LOOK

The first move Anne had to make was to take note of her own actions and try to see herself in this equation. Viewing her own behavior, she saw a tie-in with what was going on in her department. As she lost control, her staff was out of control. Each fed the other. They were locked in a power struggle and they were both losing.

Being in control does not mean keeping (or attempting to keep) the lid on too tightly. Being in control doesn't mean being autocratic. Being in control does not mean thinking only of your own needs and not of the needs of those around you.

Being in control means being aware of what is going on, and meeting the challenges with strength, resolve, fairness, and respect.

In Anne's desire to meet deadlines, she started to lose sight of her department's needs and her people's abilities. As she began to feel frustrated, she pushed too hard. The more frustrated she got, the more unhappy they got. Since they couldn't please her, they began to lose the little self-confidence they possessed. Her anger, anxiety and need to perform well were exacerbating the very problems she was trying to correct.

As supervisors, when you set up certain requirements for the job, you must know your people. To motivate them, you must understand what makes them tick. They have to feel comfortable working with you and each other. But crucial to your ability to understand others is the need to understand yourself first. If something goes wrong, you have to look at yourself first. You must understand *yourself* so that you can understand those who work with you. After you have asked yourself what responsibility you may share for negative output, then you can begin to look at others who work with you in order to find the problem. Only then can you come up with solutions for changing things to promote productivity within your staff.

What makes Anne unique is her courage to ask for help. She solved her problem by realizing she had to *look at herself first*. She changed the situation by *changing herself first*.

WHAT'S GOING ON?

There are many supervisors like this young woman: bright, capable people with too much to do, too many demands on them, unrealistic expectations for themselves and others, too few resources, and impatience to achieve results. All this adds up to too much stress. Can this scenario be changed?

It's encouraging when you meet someone like Anne who realizes that if she continues in the direction she's headed, it's doomsday. Instead of getting angry with the man who confronted her by threatening to resign, she took it as a signal to find out what was going on with herself.

When good people fail to meet deadlines, show up late for work, show no enthusiasm for the task assigned, the first step the supervisor has to take is to question himself first. Are the demands you are making impossible to meet? Do your co-workers have adequate training to fulfill the job requirements? Is your staff being rewarded extrinsically? (See Blueprint #5) If, after doing this and discovering where the problem lies, you feel your demands are not excessive, then it's time to take on the staff.

The ability to look at oneself and sort things out is the key to healthy functioning for the individual and the organization. If change is in order, then it is necessary to enter into that process. To do that, you have to ask your staff how they feel and what they would want to change to improve productivity. Some supervisors feel they will lose control if they enter into such a dialogue. Usually, the opposite is true, as people do not want to be "controlled." They want to be involved in what is going on. If you give them responsibility—ownership—you will usually find productivity levels begin to rise.

Even with that, change will be difficult. Everyone is used to doing things a certain way regardless of the outcome. As a supervisor, therefore, you will have to invest time, effort, and, possibly, money, to effect change in your organization. The important thing to remember, however, is that you, too, will have to change if you expect your staff to do so. Usually, interactions have to be examined (see Blueprint #2) to discover the underlying factors involved in poor performance.

The following is a letter from a small business owner detailing how she handled a situation when one of her employees threatened to resign. Rather than becoming angry or defensive with her, she took the following tack:

"I realized that I had better take a look at myself in this process in order to understand it correctly. Did I have to change in order to keep this employee? What did I have to do to correct things in order to keep her? Did I have to do anything? Where did the responsibility lie?

"In order to get to the bottom of this, I had to open myself up to this person and discover if I had anything to do with her decision. It took a lot of courage on my part to ask her to talk with me and tell me what, if anything, I did that brought her to this decision.

**"I was able to listen to this employee in a way I
had not done before. I made myself keep quiet and not
be defensive. I sat back, asked questions, and listened.**

**"The fact is she had many important things to say,
and by my being able to listen and not feel threatened
and worried about taking the heat, I was able to learn
a great deal about my business. I discovered that she
had legitimate concerns and I had to change the way I
was running the business if we were going to keep
good people. I discovered, thankfully not too late, that
the buck does indeed stop here!"**

By being open to change, you can enter into appropriate
dialogue with those involved. This stance is very encouraging
to people, as they see that everyone is willing to take
responsibility for change. And as difficult as change is, it can
occur when the environment supports it.

BLUEPRINT #8

CHANGING OURSELVES

INDIVIDUAL PROJECT PLANS

1.   Identify behaviors you use that are non-rewarding. What can you do to change?

2.   What is there in your everyday life that you would like to change?

   If you were to change first, what impact would this have on the situation?

BLUEPRINT #8

CHANGING OURSELVES

COMPANY PROJECT PLANS

1. Does your company need to promote change?

    Why or why not?

    If so, how?

    If not, what can you do in your department to begin the process of change where necessary?

PROJECT PLAN NOTES

BLUEPRINT #9

NO GIFT
IS SO VALUABLE
AS TIME

Do you believe that
the most valuable gift
to give or to receive is
time? From my experiences with people of all stripes, I have
noticed that there is a common thread running through
everyone's life. We complain about the very same thing: not
enough time! Everyone is running hither and yon with very
little time for reflection, not to mention time to get things
done. One of the purposes of this book is to give you some
"time out" — to read, to study and, hopefully, to reflect. Upon
reflection, perhaps you will become aware of things in your
life which you need to change and then proceed to change
them.

Not having enough time has a negative impact on the
quality of your output, your enjoyment of your life, your
behavior, your children's behavior, your relationships in every
sphere and, as a result, your productivity. Time is the scarcest
but the most valuable of resources, and yet it is squandered.
Time is the most important element in determining the
efficiency and effectiveness of the process of running a
company. While money is put into capital equipment and
technological advances, another area in which an expenditure
should be made is in training people in their use of time.

It is extremely important for executives, managers and
supervisors to be aware of the gift of time and to use it with
great skill and care. They not only determine their own
schedule but set a tone for the organization. They either

respect the use of time or use it carelessly with little regard for their own time or for that of others. Morale can be adversely affected if the people in charge show little concern for the demands of time.

If you are not aware of time as a gift, your modus operandi may be to react to matters that appear to need attention at the moment. If this is so, you are working in a very chaotic, unstructured and, unfortunately, non-productive manner. It is the classic "fire station" model of *reacting* rather than acting. If this is occurring on a regular basis, you need to ask yourself how you are using time. Then focus on your staff.

Do you have talented people working for you? If so, are you encouraging them to work responsibly and with authority? Are you empowering them to set their own agenda, take control of situations, and, as a result, add value at the end of the day?

Before you do anything, you must first be sure that you and your staff know where you are going, when you want to get there, and how you are going to do it. This type of thinking will allow you to use time more efficiently. It will help you take the clutter and stress out of your work because you will be able to prioritize and delegate responsibly. If you take control first, you will find there will be fewer crises to react to, and time will seem to expand rather than contract.

To be able to answer the above questions — where, when, and how — you need to focus on your mission statement. You and your staff need to write a departmental mission statement which fits into the company's overall mission statement. Each department should have its own agreed-upon purpose (mission) as it sets about planning its goals and objectives.

Time must be given to a scheduled weekly or bimonthly meeting in which all members of the department discuss whether they met their goals and objectives, and then plan the agenda centering on the goals for the upcoming period. To use time well, each member must focus like a laser on those goals, with the intent of doing only the work required to accomplish her mission for the following week. At the beginning of each day, everyone should set her agenda, concentrating on the completion of specific tasks aimed toward the meeting of those stated objectives. At the end of each day, each person should ask, "Did I achieve those goals?"

The weekly goals are reduced from the long-term objectives which can reach over the next year or two. By working backward from the long-range point, you determine your annual, semi-annual, quarterly, monthly and weekly goals. In this way, people learn to focus on what is vital to the company and plan time in an efficient way.

Beyond making a good product, a business has to have a good process by which the product can be made efficiently. What kind of managerial process ensures the effective use of time?

You, as managers, must make sure that you keep your staff informed, and that they stay informed on a regular basis. There must be two-way communication at all times. (Remember the ability to listen? See Blueprint #7)

The ability to trust your staff is paramount to the effective use of time. If you can begin to trust others, you will begin to know how to handle your time and respect the time of others. This will allow you to delegate responsibly. On the other hand, you cannot absolve yourself of your overall responsibility. You need to schedule time for an overview of the delegated task — for feedback, evaluation, and input. In this way, you are performing as an involved and dedicated leader, willing to empower but not to abdicate. You will be seen as someone to be trusted, and trust must be mutual if you're going to reap any reward from it.

DELEGATION

There are several reasons why executives and managers need to learn to delegate.

One, to benefit themselves by saving time and reducing the managerial load.

Two, to benefit the people who work for them, by empowering them.

Three, to benefit the company by building an infrastructure.

Appropriate delegation gives responsibility to your team and strengthens it. When you delegate responsibly, you increase the knowledge base of the company. As well, you free up your own time, which allows you to act rather than react. Delegation without adequate follow-up is "dumping", and that doesn't sit well with people. They don't want to feel they're being used. They want to be seen as integral and significant members of the team.

Delegation is not getting rid of work or overloading others. Delegation is allowing others to use and develop their skills, knowledge, and creativity in doing the task, and empowering them with the authority to act on your behalf. Without giving authority to act, you have not used time well. Delegation allows you to take the burden off yourself as you begin to realize that you are not a one-person band. Effective follow-up adds to the knowledge base of both supervisor and supervisee.

You must invest time in supervising and following through on the assignments. A time priority, therefore, must be given to all delegated work. Appropriate follow-ups must be rigorously scheduled and adhered to. These meetings must be honored, never cancelled, and allotted the time needed to fulfill your responsibility and further motivate your staff. This is time well spent and will pay off many times over. It should be regarded as an investment in others as well as yourself. In actuality, you are adding to your company's other precious resource: knowledge.

REFLECTION

The need to pace yourself, the need to take time to reflect, is essential in the use of time. The regularly-scheduled meetings with your staff are a way to reflect on the interim period. They allow you to determine not only what you did, but what you need to change.

Taking time out during the day to do nothing but think would be a wise investment in time. In this way, you allow yourself to step back as you take a breather and concentrate on something outside the office routine. You have no idea how refreshed you will feel when you return, and how much more productive you will become as a result of a brief pause during the day.

There is no magic to running a business; it takes hard work and "unmagical" principles. The principles remain the ones that keep us in focus in every area of our lives. Yes, there are techniques that you need to learn (and I'm going to talk about some of them in this Blueprint), but the key to unlocking the door to productivity is to know *yourself* and what you are capable of doing or not doing. You have to become aware of how you use this most precious gift of time. You have to look at your values — what is important in your life and what you want out of life — and realize that the passage of time may well affect your goals.

COURAGE AND CHOICES

Many times I have talked about courage in relation to so many of your actions. Courage applies whether you are an executive or not. Certainly, you need courage and the knowledge of your range of choices to get your house in order, regardless of your position in the company. To use time effectively, you can't simply learn a few techniques and hope to be successful in building productivity. While I am going to give you some information to help you understand how to manage your workload, please bear in mind that you will not be able to implement these ideas unless you have knowledge of yourself and others around you and the courage to implement change. What you are going to learn applies in whatever role you play, now or in the future. Regardless of your role, however, you will not commit to changing your ways unless you see time as a precious gift.

THE TRAIN STATION

To reduce your workload, you need to ask yourself three questions:

1. Whose problem is it?

2. Can I delegate it and to whom?

3. When is it due?

Let's take a look at the messages, memos and letters that come into your office. What do you do with all of them? How many get answered on the spot? How many get put in little piles that you plan to deal with later? ("Later" is a stressful word!) If you delay responding immediately, you are building up stress along with building up the pile of "to do" paper. Collecting stacks of things to do is the best way to feel overwhelmed. If you can learn how to disperse this paper more functionally, you will become more productive, since you will be using your time more effectively and efficiently.

Think of the "in" basket (in whatever form that is) as a train depot, and the messages or projects that go in that basket (the depot) as the trains. If you remember that a train only goes through that depot once, you'll know that you are to handle that message only once in order to decide what to do with it.

THE SWITCHING STATION

The "out" basket can be seen as a switching station. That's where the paper gets routed to its next destination. For example, if you find a piece of paper (or message) that requires an answer, you must answer it immediately. It's your responsibility as the dispatcher to get that train to the next station. The way you do that is by asking those three questions listed above:

Whose problem is it? Can I delegate it and to whom? When is it due?

The sticky part is determining, "Does this problem belong to me?" This is a question that is very rarely asked and, as a result, many managers are burdened with work that really doesn't fall into their bailiwick. Thus, they use time recklessly and indiscriminately. When something crosses your desk, decide if this is your problem. If it's not, switch it to the person to whom it really belongs. If it is in your area of responsibility, go to the next two questions: can I delegate it and to whom, and when is it due? *But get rid of it.* You now have handled that piece of paper or message only once. That train has just left the station.

You'll route papers efficiently if you set up your trains with those three questions in mind. The answers will allow you to get them to their specific destinations.

Papers you can dispatch immediately should simply go in your "out" basket. Put the appropriate person's name on each and write any necessary notations directly on the memo you received. You should also deal immediately with any e-mail, voice-mail, or telephone messages.

For all the paper that you can't dispatch immediately, you have three trains out of the depot. Two are in the form of folders, one in the shape of a wastebasket.

The train to nowhere: that's your wastebasket. Just toss those papers away.

The train to somewhere: Decide the urgency of those items, and put them in a calendar folder (one month out only) with the date you need to remove them for further action. This folder will be your tickler file for items dated for implementation.

The siding: Here you will put any items of little consequence that you do not wish to put on the train to nowhere or the train to somewhere. You will hold these for future reference. The time you go to the siding is when all trains have left the station and you have some free time to dispatch whatever is waiting for you there. Items on the siding cannot be time sensitive.

Be sure to give yourself ample time to work on your priority items, those that are important but not urgent, which are in your "train to somewhere" folder. Always err on the side of allowing *more* time rather than too little, so that your dates for action can be planned around how long it will take you to complete the project. In this way, you have created your own priority system based on when things are due and how much time is needed to complete them. Thus, you allow for interruptions, emergencies, and simply needing more time to do something than you had originally anticipated. This helps you avoid the time-crunch feeling.

Armed with knowledge of yourself and others; the company mission, plans, goals and objectives; your departmental mission statement; and your own long-term and short-term goals, you will make a knowledgeable decision about how to expedite requests. Remember, regardless of your position in the company, you are the dispatcher. You must take control of the trains that are going through the depot. You determine the train schedule, so get them out of the station on time.

THOSE PESKY JOURNALS

If you receive many professional journals, don't pile them up in a corner thinking that you are going to get to them later. (Trains should not run later!) Route them to the siding so that you can scan them when you finish with your priorities. Alternatively, if you have a secretary or assistant, ask him to go through those journals and note the articles that might be of interest or importance to your work. Your secretary can then make notations on them as to whether they are important to read immediately, or assign dates to them as to when you should read them. By involving your secretary in this routine, you also increase his knowledge of your job so he is able to participate more meaningfully. When you learn to delegate to your secretary, you begin to take pressure off yourself and, at the same time, you empower him by creating a sense of involvement, significance, and feelings of responsibility in the running of the business. In this way, you add value to the position of assistant or secretary, for the company as well as the individual.

Regardless of your role, by understanding that you only touch a piece of paper once, you won't have piles of paper around intimidating you. You decide where it goes the first time.

DISCIPLINE

You have plenty to think about in managing time because time management begins with yourself. By managing yourself effectively, you will be managing your business so that it is more productive. When you manage more effectively, you will become more efficient in your work. By becoming more efficient, you will be freeing up your time. If you develop a system that works for you — and it doesn't have to be exactly like this one — you will begin to take some of the stress out of your life. Think of yourself as a dispatcher and your office as a train station, and you will begin to switch trains onto the right track throughout the day.

Remember, too, that dispatchers need some respite during the day. So be sure to schedule a *train to reinvigoration* to leave the office at a certain time every day, and be sure to get aboard. The train should be headed for a short ride to somewhere pleasant, preferably away from the office, so you can get a breath of fresh air, smell the flowers and see the trees. Don't feel guilty. You'll come back refreshed, revived, and ready to be more productive than you would be if you stayed in the station all day.

During the days to come, ask yourself how and where you're going to receive or give this gift of time each day. If you consider time to be the most precious gift, then find joy in giving it to yourself and the people you work with on a daily basis. And if you think you'd like to receive this gift from someone else as well as be able to give it, then one day someone might just get the idea from watching you and begin to reciprocate!

BLUEPRINT #9

NO GIFT
IS SO VALUABLE
AS TIME

INDIVIDUAL PROJECT PLANS

1. Did you set up your office like a train station?

2. Check your delegation skills. In the light of what you have read in this Blueprint, how effective are you at delegating?

3. Are your goals and objectives clear, both long-term and short-term?

4. Does everything you do move you closer to accomplishing your stated goals and objectives for the week, month, etc.?

5. Do you take time for reflection so that you can gain insight into how you handle time?

6. Challenge yourself to change one thing you do each week for the next several weeks which will make your life easier.

7. How can you use time as a reward for yourself and for those you supervise?

8. On a scale of 1 to 10, with1 being the least effective, and 10 the most effective, rate yourself on your use of time.

BLUEPRINT #9

NO GIFT IS SO VALUABLE AS TIME

COMPANY PROJECT PLANS

1.   Is your company's mission statement clear? Is it the focus of your goals and objectives?

2.   Do you have a departmental mission statement? If not, do you have a plan to create one?

3.   Does your company's reward system include giving time as a benefit? If so, how? If not, why not?

4.   Does your company have in place a managerial process which ensures the effective use of time?

PROJECT PLAN NOTES

BLUEPRINT #10

SERVING THE CUSTOMER

How does a company go about motivating its customer service representatives, the front-line soldiers, to maintain needed equanimity call after call? How can a company prevent, or minimize, burnout, the stress that accompanies the type of job in which a person interacts constantly with the public? What is needed for a service representative to be as enthusiastic at the end of the day as at the beginning?

Company representatives are vital in a support role. The customer depends on them to be able to use the products sold by the company. These reps have to be knowledgeable about many products. In addition, they must be able to withstand the pressure of irate customers who want immediate service in order to expedite their own productivity.

Because of the importance of this function, I decided to send a questionnaire to the Customer Service department in one of the companies with which I had worked. The questions on the form were concerned with the level of stress felt by these representatives: how much could they tolerate, and what did they see as the company's responsibility in helping to lower it?

The following are some of the answers:

"I get very frustrated and lose perspective. I recognize there is a real person at the other end of the call who needs help, but if I get too upset/frustrated,

then I'm not objective enough to get to a solution as quickly as I should."

"I get easily frustrated and annoyed about the least thing. I work through it. What else can you do with only ten days vacation?"

"Many times when I'm home with my family, I get called in to take care of a problem no one else can handle. My wife and kids get angry, and I have no choice but to answer the call."

"Constant feeling of being uptight. Heart pounding. Lose sleep. Snappy with people."

"Headache, stomach problems. I actually had to call in sick."

"I don't think my supervisor understands what it's like to be on the phone constantly. I need more break time."

"I don't think we get enough updating on our training. I need to keep current on certain things."

"I would like to get more feedback from my supervisor. I feel as if nobody knows what I do all day except when there is a screw-up. Then everyone's at your throat."

The responses pretty much dealt with the same issue: too much pressure, not enough company support, and not enough time to balance work with family. All this makes it difficult to cope with a very demanding job.

Who is responsible for the essential function of the customer service representative? Ultimate responsibility inevitably points to the top: the policy of the company; the mission of the company; the mission of the department; the implementation of the mission; and how people in the company are treated.

Do you, as managers, ask the head of the Customer Service department what the process of customer service is and let it go at that? Or do you delve deeper?

Do you talk to the individual members of the department to discover what kind of personnel you have representing your company to the outside world? Do you take a sample of complaints and see how these were followed up? Do you ever take a survey of your customers to see how they feel about customer service? Do you, yourself, call in at periodic intervals with a complaint to see how you, as the customer, are treated?

TRAINING

In most instances, the respondents felt more training was necessary to lower their stress levels. Their feelings of inadequacy because of poor preparation in terms of product support gave them added stress when interacting with customers. At the end of the day, they did not feel as if they had been productive because of their anxiety. They also felt isolated because they lacked feedback and recognition from supervisors. Some recommended breaking the day into two separate entities: one half devoted to customer service, the other half to training or working in some other area.

Employees must be trained in human relations skills in addition to acquiring the technical knowledge they need to carry out their job. While most companies invest a great deal of their budget in computers, which are indispensable in storing and accessing information, they also need to invest money in the people who interact with the public. These people must have "the right stuff." They must be motivated to do their job with enthusiasm and understanding.

Companies that invest adequate time in training people usually have a very committed and loyal staff whose stress level is fairly low. Why? These employees feel supported, cared about, and, above all, confident in the implementation of their roles. They feel confident in meeting problems because they are trained to solve them.

Part of the training equation is to have appropriate supervisory contact available to answer questions and to solve problems. Carrying this further, however, the supervisor must heed the customer representative. If a problem has to be

solved, the supervisor must help solve it. Banalities or
tokenism do not sustain motivation; responsiveness does.

PREVENTING BURNOUT

The other area that was seen as critical in lowering stress was
in the realm of time off. More vacation time was seen as
necessary. Some suggested a four-day work week; others
suggested at least twenty-five days off per year. Others felt
angry about the intrusion of work into their home life.

In such a stressful environment, it is necessary to have
many breaks during the day, and not just coffee breaks. A
representative should be encouraged to leave her post and
take a walk for at least ten minutes at the end of every one-
and-a half to two hour period. This kind of aerobic activity
stimulates and revives.

Work-life issues have to be confronted as very real
barriers to productivity. Companies have to find ways to
redesign work schedules which would allow more balance in
people's lives. By allowing the customer representatives
themselves to confront their scheduling issues, companies
would be opening the door to greater productivity. (See
Blueprint #13)

WHAT ELSE?

Another aspect of helping the customer service representative
is the supervisor's availability and willingness to supply
positive feedback. In a day that is fraught with complaints
and problem solving, recognition by the supervisor of a job
well done is a strong motivator. The implicit message is that
management cares about you! You are an important member
of this team. As management sends this message, the
employee then sends the same message to the customer: we
care about you!

There also have to be consequences to poor service.
Weaknesses on the team must be met and managed. People
who do the same job and who are rewarded with the same pay
scale must feel that all members of the team are contributing
members. This knowledge alone lifts the level of performance.

Small group meetings of customer representatives are
necessary in order to bolster, support and create a sense of
solidarity as they share problems and seek solutions together.

It gives a team approach to their process, and they will find this very supportive as they seek to determine their own solutions to the problems that arise. (See Blueprint #13)

It is also necessary to rotate customer service representatives into other areas. This serves a dual purpose. The first one, of course, is to relieve the stress of dealing with the public on a continuing basis. The second one is for employees to be knowledgeable about all aspects of the business. There's the internal business and the external one. Everyone working in a company would do well to deal with the public, to listen to the complaints, and to understand what there is about the product that engenders dissatisfaction. On the other side of the coin is the necessity for the representative to be knowledgeable about most aspects of the business in order to be as proficient as possible in dealing with the customer.

Last but not least is the need for all employees to see possibilities for placement into different areas of the company. The way for this to happen is for management to understand the needs and desires of their employees, to be interested in them, and to convey that interest to the employees by communicating with them in a way which motivates and rewards. In this kind of environment the employee feels a loyalty which is communicated to the customer. And this makes for customer loyalty as well.

INVESTMENT IN COMPETENCE

Let's understand the term investment. Investments do not pay off immediately. Investments take time to grow and, eventually, give off the return you seek. If a company wants to be around for a long time, then it must make investments that will foster employee loyalty. People who are cared about are loyal and productive. That translates into good products and good staff. (See Blueprint #15) Furthermore, this is how a culture is built. If company reps know that the company culture values competence, the battle is usually over before it begins.

One of the themes that I explore constantly is competence. You feel competent when you are convinced you know your work. This feeling contributes to self-confidence. When you are confident, you are able to take control of yourself in such a way that you are in charge of the situation. People who feel in charge seldom have high stress levels. Competence and confidence go hand in hand.

It takes time to develop competence. We don't get educated overnight! Although this is the age of instant everything, we still can't change the fact that education is an ongoing process. For people to implement their jobs appropriately, ongoing education and training are a must.

CUSTOMER SERVICE FEEDBACK

One factor worth emphasizing is that customer representatives listen to problems all day long. They wonder, however, if anyone cares about *their* problems. One of the messages that comes through on this survey is that these employees feel that they are not being listened to, that nobody cares about them.

Merely sending out a questionnaire to this particular department made them feel someone recognized their stress and wanted to get feedback from them. This alone was energizing to them. They were telling me their problems. Was anyone at the company listening?

With highly-stressed customer service representatives, would it be to the company's advantage to take similar surveys periodically to determine the problems in that sphere and then do something about them?

STEPPING BACK

Every so often, it is necessary to step back and view the situation. That is what this survey did. It gave the respondents a chance to look objectively at themselves and their jobs.

How do you lower stress? By confronting the issues in a courageous manner and supplying solutions to problems. It isn't productive to complain. Complaining is a form of dumping, which creates its own stress. When you can determine what is creating a problem, it is necessary to ask: how can I change this situation? You then need to come up with some solutions. The solutions, not the complaints, are what you take to your supervisor. In this way, you demonstrate a commitment to your job and to the company.

It will also be to your advantage if all members of the department can brainstorm solutions. When you arrive at those that you think are beneficial to the department and to the company, you need to show exactly how the company will benefit from the proposed changes. This is taking control of the situation. This is how you lower stress and raise productivity.

If companies can implement many of the factors discussed in this Blueprint, customer service representatives will be less inclined to suffer from "battle fatigue." As a result, they will be motivated to serve the customer more effectively.

BLUEPRINT #10

SERVING THE CUSTOMER

INDIVIDUAL PROJECT PLANS

1. As a customer service representative, can you relate to the responses given in the reported survey? Which ones apply to you and your situation? How can you solve some of these difficulties?

2. How can you promote more efficiency in your department?

3. Do you feel you are recognized and rewarded in a way that is commensurate with your performance?

4. What are some of your "complaints" as a representative?

5. What can you suggest as solutions to your problems?

6. Do you feel you are given adequate, ongoing training?

BLUEPRINT #10

SERVING THE CUSTOMER

COMPANY PROJECT PLANS

1. Does your company pay adequate attention to the Customer Service department?

2. Do you as managers talk with every member of that department to find out what their problems are and seek solutions?

3. Does your company promote empowerment of these representatives so that they can do whatever is necessary to solve problems, effectively and efficiently, for the customer?

4. Who is responsible for this function in your company? Does he have a "hands-on" approach with this department? Is he available to his people? Does he brainstorm with the employees to find solutions to problems?

5. Do you take a customer survey to see how they feel about customer service?

6. Do you call in at periodic intervals to see how you, as the customer, are treated?

7. Do you have a process in place that allows your representatives to learn about other departments that are integral to the products they represent?

8. What is your company doing to redesign work schedules in order to relieve pressure and promote productivity?

9. Has your company given time to work-life issues? How are you meeting this challenge?

PROJECT PLAN NOTES

THE
CUSTOMER

'Twas brillig, and the slithy toves
Did gyre and gimble in the wabe;
All mimsy were the borogroves,
And the momeraths outgrabe.

Do you remember that? It's the first and last verse of *Jabberwocky* by Lewis Carroll. Do you know what it means? It's Lewis Carroll's language, and he is, indeed, telling us something. But what?

Do you have experiences like that during the day? Someone is talking to you but it's *Jabberwocky*! What do you do about it? Do you pretend to listen, but don't? Do you laugh even though you don't get it? Do you try to understand? Do you ask questions? Do you enter the speaker's world in order to understand?

When I deal with couples who are having difficulty communicating with each other, I often ask them to exchange shoes. As they step into each other's shoes, they actually begin to feel what the other person is all about. They can then begin to understand what the other person is saying. Only by stepping into someone else's shoes can you truly understand him or her. In this case, it is the literal stepping into the shoes. For all of us in everyday life, it is the figurative stepping-into that can lead to understanding. This understanding can be called "empathy."

The road to empathy is through listening. (See Blueprint #7) Think of how you listen to others. Are you standing in their shoes or your own? Do you wait for the first pause so that you can respond? Are you really listening, or are you preparing your rejoinder? How does this help you "connect" with the other person? Do you go after the feelings as well as the words? Do you watch and listen very carefully, so that you know what the other person is really saying?

THE CUSTOMER IS KING

In the case of Lewis Carroll's *Jabberwocky*, all we have to go by are the words. But if you heard a customer utter these words, you would have to be aware of the context surrounding them. What's the context of these words? Where do they spring from? What is the customer trying to say? While the telephone doesn't give you a three-dimensional view of the speaker, if you pay close attention to the voice, you will be able to detect if it's strained, angry or scared. If you are with the customer "in person," it is much easier to understand the message: you can watch as well as listen.

Is it your responsibility to know what the customer is saying? As long as you represent the company with which this customer is doing business, I do believe it is — even if what he's saying is *Jabberwocky*.

What do you do if the sale has already been made and the customer is unhappy? Do you listen to what the customer is saying, or do you hear only *Jabberwocky* and hand him over to Customer Service? What message does this impart to the customer? Put yourself in the customer's shoes. Imagine that you trust someone enough to buy his product instead of another person's. Then imagine that you have a complaint, but the person from whom you purchased won't listen. Instead, he sends you to another department to make your complaint. How would you feel? Would this promote customer loyalty and satisfaction? What we're talking about here is the process being as important as the product.

Companies today are stressing two things: quality and customer service. Let's get the product out with as few errors as possible, and let's do it as efficiently as possible, so that we keep the costs down. And let's make the product – or deliver the service – according to the customer's specifications. What does the customer want? That appears to be the cry today. The customer is king!

Salespeople and customer service representatives (see Blueprint #10) are usually the main contact with the consumer. A little while back, switchboard operators (that term almost seems obsolete!) were the other primary connection; but with automated answering services, the initial contact is usually a machine. Please be aware that when the customer finally gets to talk with a live person, he or she has usually been holding the telephone and pressing buttons for what seems like an eternity. Therefore, whoever is the lucky individual to come on the line as representative of the company is usually met by anger and, perhaps, *Jabberwocky*!

What is the function of salespeople and company representatives? Both need to understand the customer and deliver whatever he wants.

Who's responsible for and to the customer? The salesperson's task continues even after the sale is made. It is very important that the customer be served, nurtured, listened to and, above all, understood. This is the very same process that must occur prior to the sale. For the transaction to be a success, this service must remain in place after the customer decides to buy the product.

RESPONSIBILITY BEGINS WITH YOU
Credibility is much easier to lose than it is to gain. Once lost, it is very difficult to reestablish. A salesperson can throw away all credibility she has earned with a customer by not following through. By making promises that are not kept, a salesperson can jeopardize the reputation of the firm. With companies, there usually is no second chance.

Is it the salesperson's responsibility to follow an order through? How does a company teach a salesperson how to treat a customer? Please note that I did not say "manage" or "handle." I said "treat." You can always teach a salesperson to understand the product; she must understand what she is selling. But can you really teach a person how to "treat" a customer?

I believe you can. It starts with respect. The salesperson has to respect the customer for the customer to trust the company. That's really the formula. The respect/trust relationship is the contract that must evolve between the salesperson and the customer if the company is to survive. The salesperson is the broker between the customer and the company. She is critical to the transaction. She must be loyal to the company as well as to the customer. She needs to understand her role in caring for and about the customer. She needs to be there for the customer by walking in his shoes, so that she can key into what he is saying and feeling.

In the final analysis, given a quality product, it is the salesperson who has the power to make or break a company. How far does her responsibility go? If the customer shows that he trusts the salesperson by buying the product, then the salesperson has to continue to earn that trust by following up. In other words, if everyone took responsibility and didn't drop the ball or pass the buck, companies would run a lot more smoothly, and customer loyalty would be engendered.

HOW TO TREAT A CUSTOMER

I had a very rewarding experience with a travel agent. What differentiates one travel agent from another? Service to the customer. That's the only product they sell: their relationship to the customer. Sally, my travel agent, put together a rather complicated trip to the Grand Canyon. She made invaluable suggestions and found the lowest rates in first-class accommodations. She would scout out "packages," and never hesitate to make calls that I did not request.

Four days before my scheduled departure, Sally called to wish me a pleasant trip. She asked if I had made dinner reservations at the Canyon. No, I had not; I had never even thought of it. Sally recommended very strongly that I do so and made them for me. She said I could cancel when I arrived if I didn't wish to go. She felt, however, it was good insurance to have them. Sally went that extra mile.

Do you think I'll ask Sally to book future trips? Do you think I'll praise her to my friends? Sally built up a big trust portfolio with me by caring about me. That's the extra mile. There was no *Jabberwocky*!

A BILLBOARD REMINDER

I saw the following on a billboard:

Commit a Random Act of Kindness

I thought about this theme as part of this Blueprint. I thought about salespeople, and how very important their actions are to the company. Perhaps we can think of "kindness" as meaning "respect." Kindness to someone may simply mean thinking of the other person's needs rather than our own. Can listening to someone be considered a random act of kindness? Could we begin to transform our offices, businesses, families into safer and more enjoyable havens if we thought of our actions toward others as random acts of kindness? If the other person spoke *Jabberwocky*, and we learned to listen and understand, could that be considered a random act of kindness?

> **"Beware the Jabberwock, my son!**
> **The jaws that bite, the claws that catch!**
> **Beware the jubjub bird, and shun**
> **The frumious Bandersnatch."**

BLUEPRINT #11

THE
CUSTOMER

INDIVIDUAL PROJECT PLANS

1. If you hear what sounds like *Jabberwocky*, how do you handle it?

2. Can you think of someone who has gone "that extra mile?" Are you that person?

3. If you are in a sales position, what has this Blueprint taught you? Write down some of the ways you can serve your customers better.

BLUEPRINT #11

THE CUSTOMER

COMPANY PROJECT PLANS

1.   Does your company have training programs for salespeople?

2.   If so, what do they consist of? What do they emphasize? Do you feel they are successful? If not, how can you change them?

3.   If your company does not have training programs in place, what can you do to initiate them? What would they consist of?

4.   How does your company recognize its salespeople? What does someone have to do to earn this recognition? Is this type of reward effective in motivating people to be enthusiastic and productive in their roles?

PROJECT PLAN NOTES

BLUEPRINT #12

THE
ELAD CLUB

Are you a member
of the ELAD club?
What do you think
that stands for? Before you go on to the next paragraph, take
a guess. It's a club that's becoming more and more popular
with the fast-trackers and those people who are letting their
jobs control them. All of these high-drivers are determined to
prove that they are bona fide members of this club as they
struggle to seek admission. What do those initials stand for?
Are you a member of this elite and growing organization?

THE ELAD CLUB
This group is more widely known as the "Eat Lunch At Desk"
club. Do you continue to work as you munch away? Do you
think you are being productive as a member of this group?

When I suggest that this is not a very good practice, I am
met with all kinds of responses, such as:

**There's no way I can get my work done unless I eat
at my desk.**

**If I'm away for too long I may miss some important
call.**

**I've been doing this for years and it hasn't affected
me.**

I can't afford to lose all that time.

My boss does it, so I feel I have to.

...etc...etc...etc.

Do these excuses sound familiar? Do you recognize yourself in some of these statements? Let's take a look at some of the reasons given for belonging to this club and see if we can get to the real motivation, which is, in effect, the problem that has to be solved.

CORPORATE CULTURE

First, let's take a look at the corporate culture in which you work. Everything moves along very rapidly today. No longer is the clerk with the green eyeshade sitting on a high stool, taking his time as he dips his pen into the ink in order to write in his ledger. No, sir! We have advanced way beyond that. Today, most of you have computers at your desks, which keep you glued to your seat more than ever. You have tons of information literally at your fingertips. And with it all, you feel you are in control of your little world.

The question is, are you? If you look at some of the reasons given for joining the ELAD club, you will begin to discern an element of not being in control. If you feel so overwhelmed by your job that you can't take at least thirty minutes to have your lunch, relax, take a walk — are you in control?

If you feel that only you can answer your telephone in order to get messages, how good are you at delegating, or organizing? (See Blueprint #9.) Do you experience such stress in leaving your desk that you can't let someone else take over for a short while? If so, why? Is the answer in your organizational skills, or does it go deeper than that?

If your boss is a member of The Club, do you feel you must emulate her, even if it seems counterproductive? Ask yourself how secure you feel in your job. What do you want to achieve, and have you questioned its price?

If you're on the fast track and are intent on moving up in the organization, is The Club the route to take? What are you out to prove by joining? Do you feel it is necessary to impress others with your work habits? Is this the kind of visibility or behavior rewarded by your department or company?

OUR ENVIRONMENT

This kind of environment with its enormous pressures does not help you make decisions which can benefit you or the company. So much emphasis is put on outer display as the way to get ahead that sometimes you tend to lose track of your own values, what you truly want, and the best way to get there.

In a past edition of the Wall Street Journal, there was an advertisement which took about one fourth of the top half of a page. (Not an inexpensive ad by any means.) It was headed Working Lunch, and next to it was a picture of a man, presumably an executive, reaching over to get some ice from his very own refrigerator. The refrigerator was built like a credenza, so that the top part was a shelf, and on it were a computer and a picture of each of his children. Under this picture was the following caption:

Working Lunch
U-Line Makes It Possible — And Enjoyable

So this ad played on what is already known — that members of the ELAD club are many and growing. They may feel it's such a prestigious club that they may even want to obtain some visible status symbols, like a refrigerator that fits in next to the desk. (You don't even have to stand up to use it!).

Do you think the U-Line Corporation believes in throwing its money out on ads that won't bring results? They pegged their population: the fast-trackers who are most apt to read The Wall Street Journal. They're very much aware that the working lunch has an ever-expanding band of converts. Please note the advetisement's balm to your conscience as you choose work over family: the picture of the children on the credenza. This should assuage the guilt of anyone who belongs to The Club. You see, you do know you have a family.

THE PRICE TO JOIN

Every club has some kind of initiation fee or price to pay to join. This club, because of its exclusivity, also has a price. (I don't think it's a U-Line refrigerator!) First of all, as I just mentioned, it is exclusive. It is usually for workaholics. And workaholics come in all sizes, shapes, and motivations. You have to discover your own reasons for joining. This takes some self-examination so you can truly discern why you choose to stay in your cubbyhole when you could (should?) be enjoying yourself or the company of others in a different, relaxing environment. In this way you could recharge your batteries for the rest of the day.

Take time out now to ask some pertinent questions of yourself to see if you can find some answers. The biggest one is simply, why? *Why* do you want to join The Club?

What price does this club exact? The fellow who said he'd been doing it for years and it hadn't affected him should add the word "yet," because it does affect you one way or another. By remaining at your desk, you actually (although unknowingly) keep up the tension level without allowing it to subside. Thus you rob yourself of vitality, or upset your digestive system, either in the short run or, more importantly, over a long period. To think that this kind of unrelieved tension is going to benefit you is not seeing this behavior for what it's worth.

THE SHORT RUN vs THE LONG RUN

Many times I will talk about the ROI, the return on your investment. Investments don't have to be in financial terms. We invest in all kinds of ways and areas.

For example, when I decided to get a dog, I chose a particular breed because it appeared to answer my needs, not as a puppy, but as a mature dog. For this dog to exhibit all the beautiful qualities intrinsic to her breed, I have to invest my time and energy and a great deal of effort in training her so that she can reach her potential. I have to give of myself daily, in the short run, if I want to realize the return on my investment in the long run. I may not see any results for a while, but with time and effort, they're building.

Those of you readers who are in your twenties and thirties may not see how joining the ELAD club could possibly have negative effects. You're young, healthy, and think you've got the tiger by the tail. You can't detect any negative effects from having joined The Club, so why break off your membership?

But, as with my little dog, the results aren't in yet. Tomorrow is based on today. At forty, fifty, and beyond, we reap the return on our investment, which is based on the way we decided to live earlier.

It's very much like saving for the future through the theory of positive compounding. Those who begin their financial investment early can become very wealthy by the time they are ready to retire. They have to know what they want, plan for it, and implement an effective plan. What they put in will come out.

Is it the same with ourselves? Is it true that if you don't invest positively in yourself early on, the negative compounding effect can bring about negative consequences? Could that be what is meant by "the price you pay"? What other price is there?

Do you think you're being very productive as a member of this club? After all, you appear to make the most of your time. If you don't take advantage of every moment, it's catch-up most of the day.

The truth is, you'd be much more effective, and efficient, if you took time in your day for yourself. The reason we call it "lunch break" or "coffee break" is just that! It's a break from what you are doing, where you are sitting, what you are thinking. In other words, you need to do something different to relieve the tension and refresh you for the rest of the day.

Yes, it's true, you've changed something. You're eating. But you haven't separated. If you are in the same old place, then you have not had a break. And even if you are not aware of the problem, your digestive juices are.

Why is it necessary to be refreshed? Because tension, unrelieved, can rob us of creativity.

When we think better, we can act better.

Just take a look at the way your thought processes work at night, before you retire, and in the morning when you awake refreshed. What seemed burdensome, almost impossible, the night before now seems do-able.

With unrelieved tension, the same processes that are at work at night are at work during the day. If you give yourself a breather, a refresher, new inputs, a walk—in other words, a break—you will return to your desk feeling stimulated and ready to be far more productive than you were before you left.

THE FAST LANE

It would seem that one of the reasons for such behavior is that most people are always in a hurry. They can't seem to slow down. They do everything fast. They can't afford to eat lunch elsewhere, or take a walk, or leave their desk for periodic breaks during the day. Good gosh, no! Too much to do and not enough time to do it in!

There was an advertisement on the radio that addressed itself to losing weight fast. If you wanted to lose weight, and quickly, with no deprivation, then this particular weight loss program was just the ticket for you. If you joined this program, Z-I-P, the weight was guaranteed to melt off F-A-S-T.

The people who run this sort of program know that there is a vast population out there who wants to lose weight *fast*. If they can't lose a few pounds a week, they're not interested. There is no long-term investment in a lifestyle change, which would bring about sustained weight loss and healthy living. The fact that this type of diet is rarely successful in the long run doesn't interest them. They'll do anything to lose that weight fast. They'll drink all kinds of liquids, starve themselves over a brief period of time, and subscribe to all kinds of fad diets in their effort to beat Mother Nature. They'll do everything, that is, but change their lifestyle and invest in a long-term plan that is sound, healthy and slow.

The quicker things can get done, the better it is. Then we have more time left over for...what?

The investment in the long term is not conducive to life in the fast lane. Why? You have to slow down to achieve a proper lifestyle. You have to make an effort to be aware of your values, know what you want to accomplish over the long term and be willing to invest lots of time, energy, and effort in the short term in order to achieve it. Your value system has to include the present so you can appreciate it, and the future so you can invest in it.

In the weight department, you have to be satisfied and gratified with a small weight loss each week. You have to learn to eat the right foods and take the time to exercise. You have to spend time understanding the four food groups, the impact of fats and sugar, what a balanced meal is like. You have to learn to be consistent in your eating habits.

In other words, you have to change your behavior and your expectations. You have to get out of the fast lane.

This type of attitudinal change is very hard to come by in today's society. Today, with our emphasis on speed, where the process of doing something is second to the outcome, it's very difficult not to be a member of the ELAD club.

If you wish to resign from The Club, you need to begin to take the time to appreciate the present and realize its value to the future. You need to be as careful in how you spend your time as you are with how you spend your money.

The interesting thing to note is that we all, at one time or another, fall victim to the stressors around us. What is important is not to feel guilty if you recognize yourself in the above, but rather to be aware of the pitfalls of this behavior and begin to change. And there's no better time than right now!

BLUEPRINT #12

THE
ELAD CLUB

INDIVIDUAL PROJECT PLANS

1.   Do you belong to the ELAD Club? If so, ask yourself why?

2.   What is the price you pay to be a member of this club? Is membership worth the price?

3.   Have you tried taking several "breaks" during the day? If so, how does this time away from your desk affect your productivity?

4.   Do you feel you have a balanced life? Ask your spouse if he or she agrees.

BLUEPRINT #12

THE
ELAD CLUB

COMPANY PROJECT PLANS

1.   Does your company encourage the kind of work behavior described in this blueprint? If so, do you think this can be changed?

2.   For people to get ahead in your company, do they have to exhibit workaholic behavior like joining the ELAD Club?

3.   Is there something your company can do to discourage people from joining this club?

4.   Does your company promote work/home balance? If so, how do you implement this policy? If not, would there be merit in considering it?

BLUEPRINT #13

TEANS

Does your team or
department function
like the following? If
so, this Blueprint will put in perspective what you need to do
to get it on track.

WHAT WENT WRONG?

**This is the story of four people: Everybody,
Somebody, Anybody and Nobody. There was an
important job to be done, and Everybody was
sure that Somebody would do it. Anybody could
have done it, but Nobody did it.**

**Somebody got angry because it was
Everybody's job. Everybody thought that
Somebody would do it. But Nobody asked
Anybody.**

**It ended up that the job wasn't done, and
everybodybody blamed Everybody, when
actually Nobody asked Anybody. And Somebody
felt guilty!**

-Anonymous

All companies, basically, are composed of departments.
These can be looked upon as teams because the element of
cooperation is essential to their productivity. If you have
formalized teams, you must be able to implement the rules of
team play for members to do their job effectively.

If you have created actual teams involved in group projects, what is necessary for these teams to work? Do you assume that the "players" understand the reason each is there? Is it possible that teams can be another way of skirting responsibility? Are they a way for Somebody to do everything and Nobody to take responsibility for anything?

Some companies feel that if they put people into teams, the players on them will find their way somehow. People are used to acting in a particular way. It takes time, training, and commitment to the change to withstand the stress of the transitional period.

While companies, rightfully, want to save money, they must be willing to spend (invest) money to effect the proper training that is required to change a system. It takes time to effect change so that Everybody knows it's his responsibility as well as Somebody's in order to get the job done. This way, Anybody can be held accountable when Nobody moves into the vacuum.

Teams must decide on their goals and the role each member plays in achieving them. There has to be flexibility within the team as well as responsibility and accountability. While managers bear the ultimate responsibility, everyone on the team must feel responsibility for and to the team, as well as for his own individual part in it.

The same principles hold for a department. If, as a manager, you can prevent yourself from carrying the load and wanting to become indispensable to the business, you will begin to develop productive people. You may think you're doing the right thing by keeping your fingers in everything and being the final authority on all subjects, but you are really cheating yourself and the business. (See Blueprint #9) You cheat yourself by not respecting your own time constraints, and you cheat the business by not building a strong infrastructure so that work can progress without you. You also have a negative effect on morale, because people do not see themselves as significant or important in the business. This, in turn, limits productivity. And that's how Nobody learns to take responsibility and run with the ball.

This can be likened to the human body. If the bones are strong and sturdy, the muscles can do the everyday tough jobs of lifting and carrying, walking and running. Proper nutrition in the form of food, exercise, and rest develops a strong skeletal structure. Without the vital building ingredients, we encounter weakness and inability to do the things that make life interesting and enjoyable.

So it is with an organization. The infrastructure must be built up properly, so that each member of the company can carry the demands of the job in a way that provides cooperation, enjoyment, and profitability. To make sure you are contributing to the strength of the business, you must be aware that involvement of people through responsibility and authority leads to highly motivated employees.

Management must be concerned with morale. If you want a company to be productive, then teams, or departments, must learn to function effectively. They must be aware of and committed to the mission of the company and establish a specific mission for themselves. They must function within a structure where Everybody assumes responsibility for the job and the success of the company. In other words, the employee is committed to the company, and the company is committed to the employee.

ILLUSTRATION

Dave had been with XY Corporation for fifteen years. During all of his years with the company he worked in the factory, where he was involved in the manufacturing process. Because of his seniority and excellent work record, he had been promoted to foreman of his department. Without any management training, Dave found himself responsible for three four-man teams who worked on a machine. Each man had a specific task to do, and each one was necessary to the process.

Dave first ran into difficulty when one of the team members didn't show up for work. Dave, without consulting the team members, made a decision as to how they had to operate without the absent person. This process repeated itself each time someone failed to show up. The rest of the team members would wait for Dave to figure things out so the scheduled jobs could get done. Soon the members of the team began to complain about the assignment of added work; they did not agree with the way Dave was solving the problem. Dave would insist they do as they were told and would walk away. At the end of the day, Dave would discover that this team had not accomplished much work. This scenario kept repeating itself as Dave never changed his procedure.

One day, when morale in the department began to affect productivity, Dave's supervisor called me in to help find a solution to the unrest within the group. I talked with Dave and asked him why he didn't trust his team to figure out what had to be done in the event of a member's absence. Dave laughed derisively. That was not what they were paid for; that's what he was paid for. He determined what was going on in that department. That's why he sometimes came in at three in the morning, to make sure that all was ready for his men to do their job.

Dave felt his style of supervision was proof of his commitment to the company. From his standpoint, he was the only one who knew what to do, and he was working very hard to prove it. If Dave's supervisor were to judge his worth by the number of hours he spent on the job, he would undoubtedly be impressed by his zeal. However, Dave didn't really understand his role or the requirements of the job. He certainly was not in tune with a participative work environment. By taking over all responsibility in his department, he was preventing his teams from functioning effectively. Since Dave could not change the way he supervised, the solution was to remove him and appoint a manager who knew how to motivate his people to figure out solutions to their problems.

THE MANAGER

What is the magic in managing? There is no magic wand that makes you a successful manager. The magic is in how you treat yourself and your people, your knowledge of the job that has to be done, and how you view the process leading to the achievement of your goals.

As a manager, do you see yourself as indispensable, the one appointed to solve problems without much input from your team? Or do you see your people as consultants and encourage their input? Do you motivate your people to come up with ways to improve the quality of the process or product? Do the teams feel essential to the business, or do they view themselves as the means to an end? Do you listen to them and encourage innovative thinking? Do you make each of your people feel significant by meeting with them on a regular basis so they know their input is valued?

Does your department, or team, have a mission or sense of purpose? How does it coincide with the company mission? A specific group mission can impart a more meaningful purpose to the everyday running of a department or team. It is geared solely to that particular area and has, therefore, a presence and reality "closer to home" than the overall company vision.

TEAM COMMITMENT: A RECIPROCAL CONTRACT

For employees to feel committed to teams, the company has to manifest its own commitment. It must do this not only in training people to function within the team concept, but it must keep informed of the progress and process of the teams. Managers must meet with the teams on a regular basis for information about process and progress in meeting its goals and objectives. If a team isn't functioning smoothly, with adequate movement toward reaching its defined goals, the manager of the department must determine why and begin to enter into problem solving with the team.

Sometimes there is no synergy within the team itself. Why? Is there someone in this structure who is causing difficulty? How can this problem be solved? Does the person have to be confronted with this issue? How? (See Blueprint #14) Does he need to be removed from the team and placed in a group more compatible with his skills? Or does he work better individually, and would he contribute more to the company doing individual projects?

Then there are the managerial "teams". Are they functioning smoothly? Are managers exchanging information with each other so productivity throughout the whole company is being enhanced? Is there synergy among departmental goals and objectives? Are they cooperating or competing with each other?

Just by setting up teams, the company does not fulfill its responsibility. Managers establish accountability for teams, not by micro-managing, but by being interested and informed on a regular basis. This keeps them on track. Communication must be ongoing if productivity is to occur. (See Blueprints #6 and #9))

If teams are going to be successful, there must be mutual commitment, not only between managers and staff, but within the teams themselves. In this way Everybody will reach out and do the job that has to be done, without blaming Somebody just to avoid responsibility. In this way Nobody suffers and Everybody gains.

BLUEPRINT #13

TEAMS

INDIVIDUAL PROJECT PLANS

1. Are you committed to your company? Why? Or why not?

2. If you are not committed, what do you have to do to change things?

3. What is your role within your company?

4. Do you have teams? If so, what is your function in the team? Do you feel free to step out of the box to which you have been assigned when the need arises? If you do this, what is the reaction of your team members?

5. If you do not have teams, do you feel free to do what has to be done in your department when the need arises?

BLUEPRINT #13

TEAMS

COMPANY PROJECT PLANS

1.   Is your company committed to its employees? If so, how is this manifested? If not, what can you do to change this?

2.   What kinds of ongoing training programs do you have to help your employees function effectively in teams?

3.   On a scale of 1 to 10, with 1 being the least effective and 10 the most effective, rate the effectiveness of your team or department in its overall contribution to the company.

4.   Describe the managerial process in your company.

5.   Do you see any need to change it? If so, what would you suggest to make it more effective?

6.   Does the Illustration in this Blueprint bear any similarity to what is going on in your company? If so, what is the solution?

7.   Answer the following questions and evaluate your management style:

As a manager, do you get input from your team or do you see yourself as indispensable?

Do you see your people as consultants and encourage their input?

Do you motivate your people to come up with ways to improve the quality of the process or product?

Do your people feel esential to the business or do they view themselves as the means to an end?

Do you listen to your people and encourage innovative thinking?

Do you meet with your people, individually and collectively, on a regular basis so that they know their input is valued?

8.   Does your department or team have a mission statement? If so, how does it coincide with the company mission? If not, why not?

9.   Does your company believe in allowing its employees to help solve their own departmental problems?

BLUEPRINT #14

COMMUNICATION
AND
CONFRONTATION

"I firmly believe
corporations have life
cycles. They grow, they
prosper and, if they're not careful, they atrophy and die."

This statement was made by Philip Condit, former
president of Boeing. At the time, Boeing stressed
communication as one of the tools necessary for companies to
use effectively if they wished to continue to grow and prosper.
If appropriate communication is not fostered, corporations, as
well as relationships, atrophy and die.

In this book, you will find that a number of the Blueprints
stress communication. Each one, however, pursues a different
facet of communication. The question is: *What is
communication and how do you get it?* Is it like a disease? Do
you catch it? Do you do it naturally? Or do you go to school
and learn how to do it?

Boeing approached the topic of communication by setting
up design teams that studied companies like Ford and Toyota.
Boeing said to its employees: "You're not allowed to say,
'Airplanes are different,' because then you don't learn. As you
study these companies, you talk among yourselves in ways
which promote learning."

In other words, don't be a naysayer. Don't find reasons
not to learn something new. Even though you manufacture
airplanes, you can learn from the automotive industry. No
matter how many times you may hear something, if you are
open to learning, you will always find something new in the

message. Communication is a two-way street running between the sender and the receiver. Learn what there is to learn from companies that are successful in what they do and talk about it among yourselves. They present a wonderful model.

ILLUSTRATION

I had been working with a small start-up company. Because they had a very small staff, I stressed teamwork as one of the keys to their eventual success. I believed that if they were going to make it, they would do so only if they developed a mission statement for the company and everyone worked toward the agreed-upon objectives. They needed to discover, utilize and respect the skills of all the members. They had to be willing to communicate: listen, disagree, exchange ideas. They needed to learn from each other and work as a team in pursuit of their goals.

While this may sound easy, in truth, it is not. There's always the temptation to sit back and let someone else take the reins. When someone else is in charge and you're taking no responsibility, it's all too easy to criticize outside the forum. There's also the fear of stepping on someone else's toes, of being too aggressive and disliked because of it. Old habits die hard!

During one of our sessions, they were talking about the need to order some stationery. One of the team members had interesting ideas about designing a new look. After presenting them very sketchily, he said, "But that's not my job." (See Blueprint #13)

First lesson of the day: on a team there's no such thing as "that's not my job." If you think "It's not my job," then whose job is it?

In this case, the person did not want to usurp someone else's responsibility. How do you prevent yourself from walking on that land mine? By communicating your reluctance to take on someone else's role and then listening to the feedback. If someone feels trampled upon, then it's up to that person to speak up. Otherwise, how are you going to get things done? Communication!

The idea of the team approach is to be more efficient in getting the task done and more effective in communicating what is required. Everyone has to understand that. The objective is to get the work completed, meet stated deadlines, and reach group and company goals. The only way to do that is by working as a group—a team. Teamwork means doing the job that needs to be done by utilizing the skills of the various members of the team. All the people involved have to feel free to take responsibility and confront issues and communicate what is on their minds. It is counterproductive to confront *people*. You must always confront *issues*, so that people's sensibilities are respected and productivity isn't destroyed because of ongoing resentment.

For teams to work effectively, all members of the team must be open to learning from one another. As well, they must be willing to learn from whatever source is going to make them more knowledgeable in reaching the stated, accepted and understood goals and objectives of the team and the company. Communication! Furthermore, they must be willing to share their knowledge and their resources. With teams, the team is the star, not the individual.

Of course, friction can develop when people work together. But if you keep the goal in mind, and keep the communication lines open by the use of non-combative, non-aggressive confrontation, the team can be a very effective force in the success of a company.

CONFRONTATION

What exactly is non-combative, non-aggressive confrontation and how do you use it effectively?

First of all, confrontation is not a dirty word. It is not a negative behavior. Many people shy away from it because they do not understand it. They feel it is a very aggressive and harsh approach that is counterproductive. When used incorrectly, it can be all of these. Used correctly, however, confrontation is a method that propels groups and individuals forward. It breaks through logjams and gets things moving.

Please note that earlier I mentioned confronting the *issue*, not the person. I think the easiest and most effective way to explain this is to give you an example.

A group of technicians was sent out to solve a customer's problem with some equipment that had just been installed. After troubleshooting for about two hours, they thought they had finally found the error and proceeded to fix it. During the night, the customer called, saying that the machine was not working correctly and was causing all kinds of difficulties at the plant. The service team was roused out of bed and told to get to that plant immediately and solve the problem.

When they arrived at work the next day, the team's supervisor wanted to know whose fault it was that this had happened. No one accepted responsibility. At this point, the supervisor blasted the team and accused them of not knowing their work.

This is an example of confronting the person and not the issue. It is combative and aggressive. It sets off a whole series of negative emotions matching the bad feelings of the sender. The approach is also negative in that it does not offer a solution to the problem. The supervisor is simply venting his anger and frustration at what happened. He is not focusing on the goal of trying to discover exactly what went wrong (the issue) and not who's to blame (the person).

The group felt upset enough about what happened. If you make a mistake, you want to be told how not to get in that situation again. What went wrong? How can you avoid it in the future? If you get blasted, chances are you will feel angry rather than remorseful. Anger doesn't allow for any learning to occur; it just keeps things the way they are. Empathy, understanding, and an effort to find a solution lead to change.

If you look at confrontation in this light, as a positive approach to moving forward, you won't be tempted to denounce the person in an effort to change the act or the thinking.

COURAGE

What does it take to confront issues? It takes three things: courage, tact and empathy. Let's look at courage first.

Without courage, you cannot confront any issue. It's very difficult to stand up to someone and tell him that you disagree with either his thinking or his actions. But unless you make up your mind that the only way companies, or you as an individual, can move forward is to confront an issue, there really will be very little progress.

New information requires discussion. If everyone agrees with everyone else because of the fear of speaking out, stagnation ensues, and no change is ever made. That's what Mr. Condit means when he talks about atrophy. Atrophy occurs when nothing new is infused. Everyone just goes along her merry way, afraid of making waves and unwilling to take responsibility. No involvement or commitment occurs.

If you think of teams as cohesive groups, then you can understand the need for involvement and commitment. Without either one of these, you have no team. One of the problems that contributes to the break-up of many families is a lack of involvement with and commitment to each member of the family. There's simply too much thinking about the "I", and not enough about the "we." The same is true for teams. When you shy away from communication, you usually fear confrontation. Without appropriate confrontation of issues, there can be no meaningful communication. Without meaningful communication, you will not have a productive team or relationships. And courage is the quality that jump-starts the process.

TACT AND EMPATHY

In confronting issues, you must be tactful . Again, if you stay with the issues and not the person, you'll find you will move ahead. You will need to avoid using phrases that are accusatory: "You always," "You never," "You did." There is usually a right way and a wrong way to confront an issue, as well as a right time and a wrong time. You must be able to determine the difference, based on what you know about the situation. If you put yourself in the other person's shoes, if you empathize, you will know how to shape the words that will lead to change. By being sensitive to the other person's feelings, you will know how to present the problem. A successful implementation of this is through tact, sensitivity and empathy.

You must always be clear about what change you're trying to make. In the illustration of the supervisor and the team of technicians, the supervisor needed to find out what went wrong. His task was not to blame and humiliate. For his team to take responsibility, all the members had to feel confident that the supervisor would understand their problems. There was no need to insult them. They all needed to discuss what happened rationally, confront the issue, and discover what went awry so that they could avoid anything similar happening in the future. In a confrontation, you must ask yourself, "What am I trying to achieve?"

When you can figure that out, you will realize that by delineating the *issue* you will stand a far greater chance of achieving your goal. If you avoid the confrontation completely by not communicating at all, you will probably stand no chance of achieving what you want.

Lee Iacocca is reported to have said,

"The last year I was at Chrysler we spent $30 million on the Customer One program to teach dealers how to make customers feel at ease. But when it was over, I said, 'We're spending $30 million to tell our dealers to be polite and smile!'

Respect and courtesy: these are major components of tact and empathy. If you respect the other person, you will know how to confront an issue.

SIGNALS

When we talk about confrontation and communication, it is appropriate to talk also about lack of confrontation. This breeds its own form of indirect communication, which can wreak havoc in an organization. When I mention indirect communication, I'm thinking particularly about messages that are not answered, telephone calls that are not responded to, requests that are ignored with no reason given. These actions are a form of indirect communication; they can contribute to diminishing a person's feelings of self-worth. And yet I believe we are in the Age of Signals.

How many times have you called someone and gotten an answering device? Or E-mail? Or voice mail? You leave a message and wait for a reply. If you're lucky, you'll get a response. Otherwise, you find yourself calling again, and yet again, before you finally catch on. Nobody tells you directly that this person does not wish to talk with you. It's a signal.

Do you know the feelings such a signal can evoke? All of us have been the recipient of a signal like this at one time or another. When you don't get a response, you make a second call, thinking he probably didn't receive the message or forgot about it. After you make the second or third call, however, you get the idea. I don't think this person wants to talk with me! Then you begin to feel frustrated, inadequate, rejected. Why doesn't he want to talk with me? What's going on?

Is it being kind to avoid this sort of confrontation, or is it being cowardly and underhanded? The person who is perpetrating it feels mighty powerful in shutting someone out. But in the process, he loses credibility as an honest and straightforward person. What would happen if (heaven forbid!) the tables were turned? In business, you never know who your boss is going to be tomorrow. Where's the empathy, the courtesy, the courage?

If you don't want to talk with someone, isn't it kinder and more respectful to tell that person so directly? Then there's no questioning or anxiety. The lines of communication can still remain open.

In today's corporate world these little scenes are played out every day. Memos aren't answered; people are left out of meetings; telephone messages are ignored. These are called "signals." You see it in the newspaper all the time. The US is sending a signal to North Korea that it means business. Read the "signal" and see if you can figure out what is really meant. Or a senator is out of favor with the White House. How does he know? He wasn't invited to the latest breakfast pow-wow for the "in" group. I guess the signal means he's no longer "in"; he's "out". But nobody has actually told him in so many words that he goofed up and people in command are annoyed. We can all relate to how much anxiety that causes. How can behavior be corrected if one has no knowledge of doing something off-putting?

These are examples of lack of confrontation: indirect communication. They are the result of lack of courage, courtesy, and empathy. In companies that are spending thousands of dollars training their people in good communication skills, these examples seem paradoxical.

The route to vitality and progress, growth and prosperity, lies in a company's ability to open doors to ongoing learning, and to foster growth through effective communication and confrontation. This keeps a culture open and youthful. This keeps a company productive.

BLUEPRINT #14

COMMUNICATION AND CONFRONTATION

INDIVIDUAL PROJECT PLANS

1. Have you ever been guilty of sending signals? When? And for what reason?

2. Do you find it difficult to confront issues?

3. If you receive a signal, how can you relieve your anxiety about its meaning?

4. If you disagree with a decision, do you state your reasons, or do you go along with it? What prevents you from voicing your disagreement?

5. If you are on a team, are you aware of the goals and objectives of the team?

6. Is your team flexible? Are goals and objectives periodically evaluated so that you can change or modify them?

7. Do you feel confident in confronting issues, or are you inclined to ignore them?

BLUEPRINT #14

COMMUNICATION AND CONFRONTATION

COMPANY PROJECT PLANS

1.   Does your company culture promote or frown on expressed disagreement?

2.   Does your company believe in "signals'?

3.   What kinds of signals does it send?

4.   How does your company confront issues?

5.   Does your company embrace new ideas? Does it encourage its people to learn constantly, to stay ahead of the game?

6.   How does it communicate this to its people?

7.   Do you feel your company is vital and growing? If so, why? What does it do to communicate that message?

PROJECT PLAN NOTES

CARING

One of the routes to productivity, both personal and professional, has to do with relational skills. CARING is one of the primary relational skills that has a huge impact on the giver as well as the receiver.

A few years ago, I had the privilege of listening to a tape of General Zais, a retired U.S. Army general, giving the commencement address at the Armed Forces Staff College. The theme of the speech was Leadership Skills, and the segment on tape focused on caring. As I listened to it, I found it remarkable that a military man was giving a talk like this. It's even more extraordinary to realize that a person with such a humanistic philosophy could rise to the rank of general. He gave example after example of how a person in the military can manifest caring within a system that is not particularly noted for its consideration of the individual.

After listening to the general's message and being profoundly moved by it, I thought I would use some of his thoughts as a jumping off point for this Blueprint. Since this book is concerned with your growth, personally and professionally, the following paraphrase of Descartes seems apropos:

I care; therefore, I grow.

Without caring, can we grow? And what do I mean by "caring"? Let's first look at "valuing." How can we express "valuing" in our everyday interactions?

If you value other people, you will listen to them. Valuing other people means accepting them, not judging or evaluating. If you accept someone, you truly listen to that person. (See Blueprint #7) During an interchange, you make someone feel worthwhile, respected, valued. How he dresses, how he sounds, his manner of speech, all become irrelevant to his message. With proper listening, you will get the actual message. And with this knowledge, you, and the other person, will grow.

Listening is not just asking questions and getting answers. Listening is tuning in to the other person's very being, so that you know how she feels as well as what she thinks. It's hearing both the words and the music. Richard Dreyfuss said, you don't see a movie or hear a movie. You *feel* a movie. And it's the music that gives the movie its sense of wholeness.

It's the same with listening. You have to hear the *music* in order to feel what the other person is all about. When you are able to do that, you care. And when you care, you grow.

Caring takes time. It's not something you do on the fly. It's not something you do when someone nabs you in the corridor as you are on your way to a meeting, and you say, "OK, I've just got a minute. What's on your mind?" That kind of encounter is non-rewarding for the teller as well as the receiver. Nobody is really listening to anyone. Does this indicate caring?

You know how impressed you are when someone takes the time to listen to you. You go away thinking, "Boy, he really gave me a lot of time!" The feeling engendered is usually one of significance. "He cared about me. He listened to me. I must be OK."

If you believe that Time is your most valuable resource (see Blueprint #9), then you have to make sure you use Time wisely. Given the constraints on it, giving Time may well be a measure of our caring.

Whose responsibility is it to see that listening takes place? It belongs to both the sender and the receiver. The sender has to be tuned in to the person with whom he's talking: Is he in a rush? Is this the proper place to discuss this matter? As the messenger, you have to have an awareness of the receiver's needs. Am I talking too much? Am I listening to the response? Am I paying adequate attention to the music being played by the receiver?

The receiver has the responsibility of listening intently to the message being sent and making sure that what is said is understood. Communication is:

message sent is message received.

The way to make sure of this is to restate what the sender has said, so that both know that the message sent was the message received. To do this, you cannot be consumed with your own rebuttal or defense. If you are, you will not be listening; you will be preparing your comeback.

MANAGEMENT SKILLS

Many pieces of mail cross my desk advertising seminars on leadership and supervision. Most of these deal with techniques of management.

How do you get your meetings off to a good start?

How do you get your people to be more productive?

How do you motivate your people?

General Zais made the astute observation that when you are in school, 80% of your time is spent on learning tactics, strategy, planning, etc. In other words, you spend the majority of your time learning the techniques of management. About 20% of your time is spent on "people matters."

Once you're on the job, however, the opposite is true. The ratio is reversed: 80% of your time is spent on people matters, and 20% on the stuff you learned! Why? Because, to get a job done you have to build a relationship. You have to care about people. It's relationships that really motivate people to want to do a quality job. If you care about your employees or your colleagues, they will care about their job. Directives are not enough to motivate people.

FEAR-DRIVEN CORPORATIONS

In today's world, fear is the dominant force in most organizations. People work long hours and have very little life outside their jobs. Downsizing is a threat as merger-mania takes over. When people see their colleagues dismissed, they are worried and frightened that they may be next. Anxiety is rampant throughout the company. If employees question the company's loyalty and commitment to them, do you think they really care about the quality of their work? Or about the customer? Unfortunately, when morale reaches low ebb, it's usually "let's just do it and get on with it." Who has the time, energy, or desire to luxuriate in the pride of doing something well?

WHAT IS THE COST?

When was the last time you listened to your subordinates? Or when was the last time you felt your boss really listened to you? Does anyone really care what others are thinking and feeling? Who has time for it?

When Vince Foster, one of President Clinton's staff, committed suicide, it sent shock waves through the country. This kind of death has a tremendously powerful impact on a family, community, or organization. Everyone wonders, why? What could he have been thinking or feeling to do such a thing? At the time, President Clinton suggested that we all have to take time to be people first, to spend time with our friends and family, that work is secondary.

But in the real world, our personal lives take a back seat to our jobs. When was the last time you asked your co-worker or your direct reports about their children? Or about someone's elderly parents? Or about a single person's social life?

You may have a supervisor who comes in early, earlier, and earliest and stays late, later, and latest. Before you know it, the people in your department start to emulate this behavior. Then it becomes one of the unwritten rules of the department or company. Never mind that you're told the hours are from 8 to 5. The real hours are when the boss comes in and when the boss goes home.

Does this type of manager really care about his staff, or himself? Does he ever look around at the many people who work for him and wonder about their family lives? When do they have breakfast with their wives, husbands, or children? Do they have dinner with their families at night? When does a single person have time to shop? Do they take time out for lunch, or do they sit at their desks all day in order to impress the boss with their commitment to the cause? (See Blueprint #12) How does each company define commitment? Is it in the number of hours spent at the office, or the quality of the output and whether it is being done expeditiously?

What is the cost of this type of behavior, in quality of work and quality of life? Is this caring?

A few years ago, Fortune magazine featured on the cover a woman, who was a manager in a major company. This was the lead to a story called "Managing in the Midst of Chaos." The article presented a set of profiles of several different managers. In this woman's profile was an anecdote about her reaming out a salesman in front of others, humiliating and embarrassing him in order to make a point. The theme was that this company wouldn't tolerate that kind of behavior any longer. In other words, you had better think before you do that again, or you won't be around very long.

MANAGEMENT BY FEAR

To have such chaotic and insensitive management, there had to be chaos long before this action took place. Not knowing how to get out of this box, management now resorted to fear as a prime mover. I wonder if caring might not have been more effective.

In order to generate loyalty, isn't caring a more effective route? In order to have respect from your people, don't you have to show respect for them? Isn't respect caring?

DIFFERENT WAYS OF CARING

When I suggested to a manager that he needed to go into the factory often and show the people he cared about them, he told me he couldn't do that. Why? Because the employees might ask questions of him to which he did not know the answers.

Was that the purpose of his visits? Or was it simply to talk with his people, listen to them, and understand what they did and how they felt? Isn't that the way to build morale, by showing people you care about them? All this manager had to do was to listen to them. Listening equals caring. Caring leads to growth and forges strong bonds and relationships of substance.

General Zais said, "There is a fine line between firmness and harshness." As a manager, you must find that line, because "Human judgment, caring, is leadership."

As a manager, you are a leader. It is your task to model, to motivate, to inspire. You do so by caring about what you do as well as what others do. You do so by caring about the people with whom you interact, so that they feel a connection with you. You know that double standards don't inspire. You know that straight talk, kind but firm, is understood and respected. You know that treating people with dignity begets loyalty.

In David McCullough's book, *Truman*, he shows how a politician can be genuinely caring. Truman had respect for himself and, therefore, could respect others. He truly cared about people and did what he thought was best, rather than "political". In World War I, when he was a captain in the field artillery, he cared deeply about his men. He knew his mission was to bring them home alive and unscathed, if possible. This thought motivated his every move. As a result, his men trusted him implicitly. They knew that Captain Harry cared. He didn't have to verbalize it. He simply acted on it each and every minute. He genuinely cared, so that it was easy to implement. He became a hero to his men. They trusted him fully and were more than willing to follow his orders. They really fought the war for him. He was their motivator, their inspiration, and their cause.

ILLUSTRATION

Recently, in a very demanding and highly pressured company, Jim and Ed, two salesmen, came to the attention of Sam, the general manager of their department. The two sales men would come in at 7 a.m., read the business section of the paper, get their desks organized, and then begin their calling of clients in order to make sales. This activity went right on through lunch, which they ate at their desks, until the time they left for home, which was about 7 or 8 o'clock every night. Interestingly, their results were not as good as those of the other members of the office team whose day was not as long and stressful.

Sam was aware of the men's wearing schedule and their mediocre performance. He felt that what they were doing was counterproductive. It set a poor example for the department. Sam believed in balance in everything and cared about his people.

Finally, Sam called Ed and Jim in to his office. He suggested that they come to work at 9 each morning and leave at 5 each night. He told them to take an hour for lunch and one afternoon a week to play golf. The men were bewildered by this directive. They said their productivity would fall if they kept such a schedule. The manager insisted they give it a try for three months. If, at the end of the three-month period, their sales figures were not higher, they could go back to their old ways.

Jim and Ed reluctantly settled into their new schedule. Soon they found that they were making more sales in less time than they had when they devoted a great amount of time to their work without let-up. They also noted that they were giving more time to their families, much to their wives' and children's delight. After the initial guilt at their lifestyle change, they began to enjoy the more relaxed pace. They knew the numbers they had to meet and so applied themselves diligently during their time at the office. To their amazement, they found themselves increasing their revenue with less absolute time spent at their desks.

When they discussed this outcome with their manager, Jim and Ed agreed that they felt vitalized, refreshed and motivated, as they never had before. They projected more patience and enjoyment both in the office and to their customers, which had a positive effect on their relationships. They put more time into caring about their customers as they exchanged pleasantries along with the business of the moment. What once was a daily grind, now became a labor of love. There was balance at last.

And with balance came caring: from the general manager to the salesmen, who began to care about themselves, their families, and their customers. The results were evident everywhere.

FINAL THOUGHTS

General Zais's theme, "To be a successful leader, in the idealistic sense, you must care", should make us all sit up and think.

In caring, you must listen to the music as well as the words to feel what is happening. You need to stay in touch with people's feelings, so that you know what underlies their words. You need to be aware of the health and well being of your people and care enough about them so you can take appropriate action when necessary. If you do that, you will gain a great deal of respect and loyalty in your department. This will contribute to high morale and greater productivity. In this way, not only will you grow, but your department, company, and family will grow and flourish as well.

BLUEPRINT #15

CARING

INDIVIDUAL PROJECT PLANS

1. How do you show caring to yourself, your family, and your co-workers?

2. Do you feel your life is in balance? If not, what can you do to change it?

3. Do you feel you are successful in your job? What traits or qualities do you have that helped you succeed?

4. Do you see yourself as a caring individual? What brings you to this conclusion?

5. Do you subscribe to the 80-20 rule as described by General Zais?

BLUEPRINT #15

CARING

COMPANY PROJECT PLANS

1. How does your company show it cares about its employees?

2. As a department head, how do you show you value your people?

3. Do you believe you and your company are seen as caring?

4. Does your company subscribe to work/life balance? If so, what are some of the ways you promote this concept? If not, what can you do to implement this practice?

5. Do you see your employees as loyal to your company? If not, what can you do to promote loyalty among your staff?

PROJECT PLAN NOTES

PROJECT PLAN NOTES

QUALITY: FROM THE ORDINARY TO THE EXTRAORDINARY

In Anthony Robbins's book *Unlimited Power*, he says: "There are strategies for financial success, for creating and maintaining vibrant health, for feeling happy and loved throughout your life. If you find people who already have financial success or fulfilling relationships, you just need to discover their strategy and apply it to produce similar results and save tremendous amounts of time and effort. This is the power of modeling. You don't have to labor for years to do it." (Robbins, 1986, p. 112)

How many companies follow that advice? How much time, effort and money are spent "rediscovering" what is already known? Do people take the time to look around to enrich themselves by modeling?

What or who are your resources? Do you ever consider successful people as your resource bank? For example, if you have an outstanding salesperson, do you aim to discover what she is doing, and then have her teach the rest of your sales staff to do the same thing? To reinvent the wheel is costly and non-productive. Furthermore, to have your people share their winning strategies with the rest of the staff is one of the best routes to a productive company.

Without appropriate appreciation of these successful people, modeling of unsuccessful ones can also take place. That is how a culture is created. If the company culture is known to value and reward productivity, then these successful people become our role models. If, on the other hand, productivity is just taken for granted, not remarked upon or appreciated, then others see no reason to emulate the productive ones. The prevalent attitude quickly becomes, "It doesn't matter what I do, no one notices anyway." Is this productivity? Does it encourage Quality?

In a culture that rewards ideas and creativity, the role models are in place. How can we use our knowledge of their success to help our company and ourselves? Since they've already been there, let's not reinvent the wheel.

If you learn to use modeling, you will save a lot of time and enhance your efficiency. For example, when you have satisfied customers, have you ever stopped to analyze why they're satisfied? What has been the interaction between you and the customer that has produced such a Quality relationship? Quality relationships don't just happen! They are the result of positive interactions.

One of the reasons businesses begin to flounder is that people take good relationships for granted. These may be relationships with the internal customer or the external customer. Businesses stop interacting effectively with their employees (they think they'll remain forever), and they don't continue whatever they're doing to continue to nurture satisfied customers. They think they'll remain forever as well. In other words, we tend to think tomorrow will be just like today, no matter what we do. We forget that Quality requires constant awareness and effort. Because you have achieved Quality today doesn't mean you will always manifest it.

In many companies, particularly with restructuring so common, the older, more experienced people are being let go. These long-term employees were aware of studies that had been done, processes tried that led to successes as well as failures. Without this resource, a company can find itself wandering around in the dark and repeating studies that have already been undertaken.

If you find you can no longer afford to keep the older employee on your payroll, you might want to consider how to utilize this resource in another way. Consulting? Teaching? It would be in the company's best interest to create any niche that would allow that knowledge base to continue being tapped. One of the interests this would serve would be to model to the remaining employees that the company cares about people. When a company is not perceived as discarding long-term employees like so many pieces of paper, there is less anxiety among its people. It's natural for employees to identify with those who have been with the organization a long time. They begin to wonder whether what has happened to others will happen to them. As they note the company's appreciation and utilization of long-standing, loyal and knowledgeable people, those who remain will become loyal to the company in ways that will serve the company well. In fact, they will prepare themselves to step into those roles when their time arrives. Productivity in spades!

One of the jobs of management is to be aware of the good performers in the organization. Rather than give "employee of the month" awards, which have their negative as well as positive aspects, would it not be better to discover what these employees do that makes them successful at their jobs? We jokingly talk about "bottling" success and "selling" it. Perhaps one way to do this would be to have these employees teach what they do, so the rest of their division can learn how to emulate that success painlessly and cost-effectively. Does a company want to have success personified in a few people, or in many?

Many companies periodically send their staffs to seminars or workshops. Why? To increase their knowledge base? What happens to this added knowledge once these employees return? Does the organization take advantage of this input? Does it set up some system whereby the new information can be shared and discussed among the staff? Does it maximize its investment through the effective use of communication? How can this method change an ordinary company to an extraordinary one?

It may not be necessary for companies to spend a lot of money to find answers to their problems. By looking objectively at the situation, they can discover what they already have. They might be surprised to learn that the expenditure of money is not the solution to their difficulties. In most instances, problems can be solved simply by utilizing the resources you have within your organization to effect positive change within the company. Your resources are your people. The more flexible and adept your company is in communicating with all the employees, the stronger your organization will be.

This kind of thinking calls for trust, openness, and flexibility inside the organization. It promotes the empowerment of the employees. They are encouraged to think, to look around for ideas about how to create a more productive workplace. This type of thinking is necessary to highly productive and efficient teams. All this adds up to Quality.

There needs to be a concerted effort on the part of management to strive for those elements of Quality throughout the company, if customers are to receive Quality in the service or product that they buy.

COMPANIES ON ALERT

Once companies have satisfied customers, do they rest on their laurels? Do they think their customers will always be loyal to them? Even marriages in which the partners promise to love, honor and cherish each other have to be alert to the changing needs of the relationship. What worked at age twenty or thirty will not produce a Quality relationship at fifty or sixty. Needs change. People must be aware of the world around them as well as their own inner world to keep up with the changes. What makes for successful companies? Effective strategies and an ongoing analysis of good relationships with both the internal and external customers, with the goal of perpetuating them, are fundamental needs in business,.

The basic strategy of any company or relationship is to stand at a little distance, look around, and see what is going on. By acknowledging that things are always changing, kinetic, never static, you will always be ahead of the pack. If you realize that all the eyes and ears of your company are necessary to its success, you will be making use of the talent within your sphere of influence to promote productivity. You need not reinvent the wheel. Everything you want to know is more than likely at your fingertips. All you have to do is look, listen, and have systems in place by which knowledge can be transmitted.

BLUEPRINT #16

QUALITY: FROM THE ORDINARY TO THE EXTRAORDINARY

INDIVIDUAL PROJECT PLANS

1. What are your personal resources? Is your company making full use of these?

2. Do you see yourself as "successful" in your company? If so, are you aware of your modeling this behavior for other members of the staff? Do you see yourself in the "mentor" role for new hires?

3. If you are sent to a seminar, what do you do with the information when you return? For yourself? For others?

4. Are you personally aware of changes you need to make to stay abreast of the latest thinking in your field?

BLUEPRINT #16

QUALITY: FROM THE ORDINARY TO THE EXTRAORDINARY

COMPANY PROJECT PLANS

1. Does your company utilize to the fullest the knowledge of the employees? If so, how? If not, how can you change this process?

2. Define your company's culture. Is it in harmony with the message in this Blueprint? If not, what can you do to change things?

3. If your company encourages employees to attend seminars or workshops for enrichment, what system do you have to inject this new information into the company?

4. On a scale of 1 to 10, with 10 being the highest and 1 the lowest, rate your company on each of the following traits: trust, openness, flexibility.

5. Does your department take time periodically to review the changes that are necessary for quality and productivity? If not, what can you do to institute such a procedure?

6. Define what Quality means to your company.

7. Do you consider your relationship with your internal customer a quality one? On a scale of 1 to 10, with 10 being the highest and 1 the lowest, rate the quality of this relationship from your perspective.

8. Do you consider your relationship with your external customer a quality one? Do the same on this question as called for in #7.

PROJECT PLAN NOTES

PROJECT PLAN NOTES

RESTRUCTURE AND REORGANIZATION

Downsizing appears to be the buzzword of the day. Every time you pick up a newspaper you read that a company somewhere is undergoing change. It is "restructuring" either because of low productivity levels or as a result of takeover. With all this change going on, there is much uncertainty in the world of business today: uncertainty about the future, uncertainty about jobs in the newly constituted company, and uncertainty about company identity. Do these changes reduce rather than enhance efficiency?

What happens to companies that undergo restructuring? At first, productivity usually falls off, as stress levels of the employees reach a state where performance is hampered. Morale is usually affected as people wait around for.... what?

How can productivity be helped in the face of such tension? Companies are people, and people everywhere feel threatened by change. Once that is understood and accepted by management, management must then be sensitive and responsive to the staff. It is only then that change and the threat of change can be dealt with.

As people read about downsizing, they are afraid that their company, too, will end up with this "disease." Since high morale is one of the keys to productivity, the question that needs to be asked is whether high morale is possible in this climate of uncertainty. Once anxiety about being downsized enters the workforce, morale, and thus productivity, is usually affected. Given this situation, how can managers maintain a feeling of security and safety among their people, as well as within themselves, so that productivity remains high?

In times of crisis, the most natural thing to do is to "hunker down." This implies business as usual, which means not talking about what is uppermost in people's minds. This is the exact opposite of what needs to be done in order to promote productivity. The possibility of change must be met by talking about it, by communicating from the top down, from bottom to top, and laterally. Employees must be encouraged to ask questions of their supervisors, and supervisors must feel it their responsibility to answer. The type of communication that embraces questions and answers, truth and honesty, promotes trust. It lowers, not raises, the anxiety level. Although it is time consuming, it needs to be seen as an investment. By taking the time to communicate in this way, companies will become more productive rather than less.

Many times, people feel that if they don't know something they can manage much better. That is a myth that must be debunked. Not knowing is far more stressful than knowing. If you know, you can deal with it. Not knowing causes anxiety, and anxiety lowers productivity.

Managers need to overcome fear and anxiety about carrying on sensitive dialogue with employees. This leads to openness and trust. Once you ask for opinions, you must be prepared to listen to them and, whenever possible, to act on them. If there are reasons you cannot implement an employee's suggestion, then you need to spell them out.

In times of tension, executives are usually incommunicado. An air of crisis pervades the company as managers are seen busily meeting among themselves. Such an atmosphere has a negative impact on productivity. Employees tend to become very anxious as they see management in combat mode. What's going on? No one is talking!

Communication of an open sort, where management is available to its employees, is mandatory in day-to-day functioning. If openness and trust are nurtured within a company, change can be effected more easily than if these are absent. In other words, if the foundation of trust is already in place, the challenge of change can be met more positively.

However, even in open companies, change is challenging to the individual and the company. Change represents a loss of the familiar and consequences of an unknown variety. Therefore, in times of crisis, it is particularly important for management to be available to its people and to answer questions as honestly as possible.

In any company, the leaders must make decisions. Sometimes it is not in the best interests of the company to allow participation in particular decisions. Some areas are only for senior management. But some kind of communication must occur that will cut through the tension being fostered by change. Stress levels are lowered when company goals are clarified, and the employee's place within the system is understood. If some employees are to lose their jobs, then this too must be clearly explained.

When two companies are to merge, do people see this as threatening to their jobs? Do employees perceive differences in the style of the two managements? Is there a culture clash? (Think of IBM and Lotus! Or Chrysler and Daimler Benz!) Do senior managers assure their people that they have a master plan for the changes that are to take place? This kind of action not only lowers the stress of the rank and file employee, but of management as well. People feel they have some control of the situation.

These are issues that must be met head-on by management if the company is going to remain productive during a crisis of change. What can you, as a manager, do to help prepare your staff in the event of downsizing? Actually, much of what happens in a crisis is based on what has happened in the past. The management style exhibited over time will have enormous impact during a crisis of change. If the communication that occurred in the past was positive and open, it will bear fruit during difficult times.

If your performance reviews have been frequent, detailed, and honest—if you have communicated with your direct reports exactly what they do well and what they need help in—you will have done much to develop trust. If someone was not performing up to standard, did you communicate this fact to her? Did you then check up at a specified time to see if the solutions agreed upon were forthcoming? This is where many managers fall down. Confrontation and communication are not their strong suit.

If a person's performance was not up to standard, did you keep him around so that he became part of the "deadwood"? Did you feel you were being kind to this employee? If this person is not adding value to the company, in crunch time no one will want to find a place for him. Managerial inaction does not serve anyone well. If you develop a reputation as a straight shooter, you will be better able to weather a downsizing crisis with your staff.

Did you encourage your staff to develop many areas of knowledge? Were you willing to offer a person a move to another department to enhance his know-how? Does your staff see you as generous in allowing self-improvement courses? Have you mentored your people so that they know you have their interest at heart?

Do you know your people? Do they know you? Have you developed a bond with your staff and given them responsibility so that if they are outplaced, they will know they are worthwhile and have the ability to get another job?

Have you taken your own advice by keeping yourself up-to-date and knowledgeable about as many areas as possible in your company? Have you kept up with innovations in your profession? You need to be adept in your own field, but you also need to know and understand what your staff and others are doing.

The most important aspect of restructuring is based on a company's track record. If the foundation is in place, employees will feel less anxiety as they will have developed a bond of trust with the company. While restructuring is not a pleasant task, and some people will lose their jobs, companies which have invested a great deal in employer-employee relations will weather this crisis more positively than those who haven't. It is never too late to put all the bricks in place in case the unthinkable does happen. Take an inventory of your company, your management, and yourself within that galaxy. What do you have to do to prepare for the crisis of change, both as a company and an individual, if and when it occurs?

BLUEPRINT #17

RESTRUCTURE AND REORGANIZATION

INDIVIDUAL PROJECT PLANS

1. What can you do to prepare yourself in the event of downsizing?

2. Evaluate the process of your performance reviews. On a scale of 1 to 10, with 10 being the highest and 1 the lowest, rate their overall effectiveness in helping you reach your goals and objectives.

3. On a scale of 1 to 10, with 10 being the highest and 1 the lowest, rate trust and openness between you and the management.

4. Have you developed your skills in many areas, so you will be able to move into another position if the company eliminates your job?

BLUEPRINT #17

RESTRUCTURE AND REORGANIZATION

COMPANY PROJECT PLANS

1.   What do you do, as a manager, to develop trust within your staff?

2.   Take a good look at how you implement performance reviews. Are they given a priority in your company? How often are they done? What do you need to do to change to make them more effective?

3.   Do you have people on your staff who can be categorized as "deadwood"? What are you going to do about it?

4.   How many people have you sent to "improvement" courses in the last six months? What do you do when they return? Do you have them share their knowledge with you and the staff? Do you attempt to implement changes as a result of what they have learned?

5.   What do you do in order to know your staff? How do you develop a feeling of trust?

6.   Are you aware of what each member of your staff is doing? Do you plan regularly scheduled meetings in order to keep current and give feedback?

7.   Have you taken an inventory of your company, your management, and yourself? What do you need to do to prepare for a crisis of change?

PROJECT PLAN NOTES

BLUEPRINT #18

"PLAY YOUR OWN GAME"

"Play Your Own Game" is a theme that caught my fancy from a little gem of a book called Quantum Golf, by Kjell Enhager. While the author teaches you how to play golf by relaxing and enjoying the game, he is also teaching you how to play the game of life. One of the most salient bits of advice he offers the reader is to Play Your Own Game.

Is it possible to do this in the corporate arena? Or in your family? Or with your friends? Let's take a look and see whether or not you can follow this counsel.

In many Blueprints, I talk about the management of yourself to help you become more productive. When you learn to manage yourself in your use of time (see Blueprint #9) by taking control of the paperwork and E-mail that comes your way, by delegating responsibly, by taking time during the day to relax and exercise, you will begin to find you are more productive. You will breathe more easily and feel the lifting of the stress that encumbers you. This is just the first step toward taking control of your life, both at the office and in your home. Your office impinges on your home life, and vice versa. If you can keep your head above water at the office, you might be able to come home more relaxed and ready to enter into your family life with anticipation of pleasure and true involvement. If you do what many of the Blueprints suggest, I believe you will be well on your way to playing your own game.

Many people express frustration and uncertainty about taking charge of their own lives. They say, "We know our lifestyle is pretty grim. We know we elect not to take vacations, or, if we do, we are apt to be on the telephone with the office daily. We know we work long days. We know we are caught up in our jobs, to the detriment of our family and our personal lives. But let's face it, do we have any choice in this? Do we have the power to change things? Short of leaving our jobs, how can we take away the pressure of all the demands?" In other words, how can you play your own game?

CHANGE AND CHOICE

How can you change the situation in which you find yourself? What are your choices? How do you arrive at the place where you can truly identify those choices?

First of all, to lower stress it's absolutely necessary to feel you have choices. And to have choices, you have to know where you're going and what you wish to accomplish. You must have goals. Without goals, it is very difficult to change a situation effectively.

GOALS

Having goals simply means knowing what you wish to achieve, both personally and professionally. The other half of the equation, and equally important, is knowing when you would like to achieve it. There are short-term goals and long-term goals. Your long-term goals help determine where you want to be at a specific time in your life. Your short-term goals are benchmarks along the way. If your short-term goals are on target, you will be motivated to continue.

How far away should your long-term goals be? Your age plays a big part in that determination. Where do you want to be and what do you want to accomplish by the time you are 40, 50, 60, 70? Is this too far out for you? Then narrow it down to where you feel comfortable, but don't be shortsighted. One of the biggest causes of regrets is the "I should have" syndrome: not looking far enough ahead, and then letting time slip by so that you reach a point without knowing how you got there.

If you don't know where you want to be, how will you know where you are going? Furthermore, if you don't know where you are going, how do you know what you have to do to get there? In other words, how can you play your own game?

ILLUSTRATION #1: JACK

A few years ago, Jack, a man in his early thirties, came to see me. He said he was suffering from "burnout." He felt directionless, unmotivated, and couldn't seem to find the energy to finish his tasks. Life seemed to be overwhelming him; he couldn't find much joy in anything.

He was married, with two small children. Besides holding on to a responsible job during the day, he was taking courses toward an MBA two nights a week. Going from early morning to late at night, he arrived home too late to see his children. He wasn't eating or sleeping well as he couldn't release the tension he was feeling much of the time. Given all this, is it surprising that Jack was experiencing "burnout"? Not an unusual condition under the existing circumstances.

When I suggested he had set this up for himself, he was quite shocked and surprised. He felt he had no choices and no control over his situation. Jack felt like a victim, powerless to change things.

To understand Jack's behavior, we need to delve somewhat into his background. When Jack, an only child, was fourteen years old, his father had died. Not having a lot of money, his mother went to work to make sure Jack would not be deprived of an education. Jack's only task was to concentrate on his studies and do well academically. At his mother's urging, he went to college, pursued a business degree, and graduated. After college, he got a good job and had been employed ever since in the same company. When promotions didn't come his way, Jack decided to work towards an MBA degree. He thought if he had that credential, he might advance. He was determined to make his mother proud of him, as he felt this was a debt he owed her.

Did he enjoy the work he had chosen? Not exactly. What were some of the things Jack really liked and did well? His face lit up as he talked about carpentry. It seemed he was quite good at this and loved to build things. His mother discouraged him, however, as she considered this pursuit "blue collar." She said she hadn't worked all those years to see her son do such "menial" work. Jack, feeling obligated to his mother for caring for him and sacrificing for him, did as she wanted and never openly questioned the decision he had made about his career.

When I suggested that the decision was his mother's, not his, he was taken aback. No, no, this was what he wanted to do. What were his goals in getting his MBA? Finding a better job. What kind of job did he aspire to? It didn't make any difference, since he had no strong likes or dislikes; he just wanted to gain more status in his company and make more money. Why? Because he felt that was the measure of success. If he had a more prestigious job and made more money, he could prove to his mother that she hadn't made all those sacrifices for nothing.

Whose game was Jack playing? His own, or his mother's? What did he owe to his mother? What did he owe to himself? How was he going to overcome his feelings of despair, if he didn't begin to play his own game?

ILLUSTRATION #2: JOAN

Joan was a single woman in her twenties who had recently moved to the city to work with a new company. Since she had moved to this location from quite a distance, she found herself adjusting to her home and job at the same time. She was eager to do well in the company and she also had a great need to make friends.

After work, as a way to relax and socialize, Joan's co-workers liked to frequent bars. In order to gain acceptance by the group and feel part of their social network, Joan agreed to go along, although she didn't like to drink and felt she couldn't afford the money it took to keep up with this game.

After a few months, this routine began to disturb her. While she wanted to be part of the social scene, she found herself struggling to conform to a lifestyle she found in conflict with her values. When evening came, she felt "tied up in knots" as she continued to play the game.

When she began to experience stomach pains and digestive difficulties, she visited her physician. He could find nothing wrong with her physically and suggested she see a psychologist as he felt her discomfort could be caused by stress.

Was Joan's desire to belong, no matter the price, causing her tension? Was there a conflict within her as she struggled to be part of the group? Was she looking at her problem and figuring out what her choices were? Was Joan playing her own game?

ILLUSTRATION #3: RALPH

Ralph's problem revolved around his boss and his co-workers. In every company, there are written and unwritten rules. The written ones are simple to follow; the unwritten ones usually have to do with a culture that has sprung up within the company. These are very difficult to battle. It's like swimming against the tide.

When Ralph joined the company, he was told that working hours were 8 to 5. He was a salaried person, so he gained no additional compensation by working overtime. Ralph had three young children and would help his wife, who also worked, get them ready for school in the morning. He also looked forward to returning home in the evening to have dinner with his family, which he found very relaxing and enjoyable.

As Ralph settled into his job, he noticed that he was always the last one to arrive and the first to leave, even though he was never late in the morning and left shortly after five most nights. Soon he began to feel that he was doing something wrong, but he didn't know what.

After some sleuthing, Ralph discovered that his boss was at his desk every morning at six o'clock and stayed until after seven every night. To his chagrin, he also learned that the people working with him struggled to get in earlier than the boss every morning, and to leave with him every night. Ralph began to realize that he was not part of the loop. He also found that his boss believed the number of hours an employee spent at his desk determined his level of conscientiousness, the quality of his work, and his commitment to the team. Soon Ralph was coming in at 6:30 and leaving after 7.

Was Ralph happy with this arrangement? His family life began to suffer as arguments with his wife became more frequent. He had no time to work out and very little time to be with his children. The constant stress at home and the office began to take its toll both physically and emotionally.

Did Ralph believe he had any choices? Was it possible for Ralph to play his own game?

LEARNING TO SAY NO

Jack, Joan and Ralph all had a hard time saying, "No." They didn't realize they were playing someone else's game.

Jack felt so burdened by obligation that he just limped through life, putting away his own dreams and desires in order to pursue his mother's. Joan so desperately wanted to be part of the crowd that she forgot there was a price for struggling too hard to become what you're not. Given Ralph's lifestyle preferences and his boss's measures of quality, Ralph never stopped to ask himself whether he was in the right department or company.

None of them considered whether there was a conflict between his or her value system and the values of others. They never stopped to ask themselves whose game they were playing, and whether the rules of others were the ones with which they could comfortably comply.

There are many stories like Jack's, Joan's, and Ralph's – different twists and turns, but the same type of scenario. We find people doing things for reasons, conscious or unconscious, which don't allow them to play their own game.

Stand back and ask yourself what you wish to accomplish in life. Are you headed in that direction? Sometimes you may get bogged down by materialistic demands, ambition, or social pressures. As a result, in order to achieve your goals, you may end up playing by someone else's rules. Is that playing your own game? Perhaps, because pride demands that you move to the next step on the career ladder, you fail to ask yourself what you really want, in the long term as well as the short term. Will that next step lead you to what you want out of life? Have you defined your values? Are you playing your own game?

If you don't enjoy going to work in the morning; if you feel dragged out and tired each day; if you look forward to nights and weekends when you can indulge yourself in doing things you love; if you find you're not enjoying life and you have no clear-cut goals or direction, then you have to ask yourself whether you're playing your own game.

Is it possible to play your own game in every situation? If you are experiencing conflict, have you identified the opposing forces? Rather than seeing your life in black and white, can you arrive at a compromise where you can play the game with more flexible rules? In carving out a niche for yourself based on the reality of the situation, you will begin to satisfy your own needs while being a productive member of a company.

As you learn to put limits on others' demands of you, you will work wonders in relieving your stress factor. If you do your job well and are genuinely interested and involved in what you do, take time for yourself and your family, you will have begun to take control of your life. In this way, you will not only be more productive in every facet of your life, but you will be playing your own game.

BLUEPRINT #18

"PLAY YOUR OWN GAME"

INDIVIDUAL PROJECT PLANS

1.   Ask yourself whose game you are playing. Do you know the art of compromise?

2.   Do you have a personal mission statement and specific goals and objectives? If so, what are they? If not, think about writing some.

3.   Does your mission complement the company's mission?

4.   What are some of the things you might be doing that you would like to stop?

5.   Put yourself in Joan's shoes: what could she do that would not conflict with her values and still allow her to be part of the group?

6.   Put yourself in Jack's shoes: what could he do that would allow him to play his own game?

7.   Put yourself in Ralph's shoes: what could Ralph do to satisfy both his personal and professional needs? What are his options for compromise?

BLUEPRINT #18

"PLAY YOUR OWN GAME"

COMPANY PROJECT PLANS

1.   What are some of the unwritten rules in your company? Do you subscribe to them?

2.   Describe your company's culture. If you, as a manager, are not pleased with it, how can you begin to change it?

3.   Does your company promote open discussion of the issues of work/life balance?

4.   Is it possible to play your own game within the company environment? If so, will this have a positive or negative effect on personal and company productivity?

PROJECT PLAN NOTES

DR. EILEEN L. BERMAN

Dr. Eileen L. Berman, a licensed psychologist, has practiced clinical and corporate psychology in both the U.S. and Australia. She has consulted with hundreds of senior and middle-level managers in a wide range of organizations, from family-owned businesses to large multinational corporations.

Prior to her tenure in Australia, she was a psychologist at the Fallon Clinic, Worcester, MA; a consultant to Worcester Academy; and Adjunct Professor of Education and Psychology at Assumption College Graduate School and Worcester State College.

For ten years, Dr. Berman wrote a monthly column on stress and productivity for *Business Digest* and also published the *CEO Growletter*. The *Growletter* focused on creating employee optimization and was read throughout the U.S., Australia, Japan, and India. At present, she writes a monthly column for *Industrial Management* magazine.

Dr. Berman's first book, *You're Fired! A Unique Approach to Rebuilding Your Life*, was published by Engineering & Management Press in 1998.